P9-CLR-257

# HINDENBURG

*MILITARY PROFILES*

**SERIES EDITOR**

*Dennis E. Showalter, Ph.D.*
*The Colorado College*

*Instructive summaries for general and expert*
*readers alike, volumes in the Military Profiles*
*series are essential treatments of significant and*
*popular military figures drawn from world history,*
*ancient times through the present.*

# HINDENBURG

## Icon of German Militarism

*William J. Astore and Dennis E. Showalter*

*Potomac Books, Inc.*
*Washington, D.C.*

*Library of Congress Cataloging-in-Publication Data*

Astore, William J.
    Hindenburg : icon of German militarism / William J. Astore and Dennis E. Showalter. — 1st ed.
        p. cm.
    Includes bibliographical references and index.
        ISBN 1-57488-653-3 (hardcover : alk. paper)—ISBN 1-57488-654-1 (soft-cover : alk. paper)
        1. Hindenburg, Paul von, 1847–1934   2. Presidents—Germany—Biography.   3. Generals—Germany—Biography.   4. Militarism—Germany—History.   5. Germany—Politics and government—1871–1933. I. Showalter, Dennis E. II. Title.

DD231.H5A8 2005
943.085´092—dc22                                                     2004013454

(alk. paper)

Potomac Books, Inc.
22841 Quicksilver Drive
Dulles, Virginia 20166

first edition

10 9 8 7 6 5 4 3 2 1

# Contents

|  | List of Maps | vii |
|  | Preface | ix |
|  | Chronology | xiii |
| Chapter 1 | Prewar | 3 |
| Chapter 2 | The Eastern Front, 1914–1916 | 15 |
| Chapter 3 | Supreme Command, 1916–1917 | 39 |
| Chapter 4 | Collapse and Catastrophe, 1918 | 53 |
| Chapter 5 | Weimar and Hitler | 77 |
|  | Epilogue | 101 |
|  | Notes | 106 |
|  | Bibliographic Note | 120 |
|  | Index | 127 |
|  | About the Authors | 133 |

# List of Maps

*Tannenberg*, 1914                                      21

*The Ludendorff Offensives*, 1918                       64

*Europe in* 1924                                        85

# *Preface*

To the historian Hans Delbrück he was "the great old zero." To Adolf Hitler he was "the old cab horse." In many histories of World War I, he appears as a slow-witted figurehead dominated by a dynamic, innovative, and excitable Erich Ludendorff. For most Americans his name conjures up images of the eponymous dirigible that in 1937 exploded spectacularly in flames. Yet, to millions of ordinary Germans during and after World War I, Paul Ludwig Hans Anton von Beneckendorff und von Hindenburg was the hero of Tannenberg and an icon of such Prussian virtues as discipline, duty, order, and respectability. From the crucible of war, he emerged as an *ersatz kaiser:* a symbol and substitute figure in the imperial role Wilhelm II could not fill and Weimar politicians could not replace.

Hindenburg's life encompassed and encapsulated the Second Reich's rise, collapse, and rebirth as the democratic Weimar Republic, an entity weakened by economic dislocation and depression and eventually overwhelmed by the thrusting militarism, hypernationalism, and racism of Hitler's National Socialist German Workers' Party (NSDAP). Today, Hindenburg's reputation is irredeemably stained by the role he played in facilitating Hitler's legal acquisition of power, with the Prussian field marshal reduced to the Bohemian Corporal's *Steigbügelhalter* (stirrup holder).[1] Once in the saddle, Hitler proved impossible for Germany to unhorse. By entrusting the reins of government to Hitler, Hindenburg in 1933 precipitated "an earthquake shatter[ing] 66 million lives."[2]

Like Hitler and millions of other Germans, Hindenburg was transformed by World War I. After a successful, if unspectacular, military career spent largely in peacetime routines, destiny was thrust upon Hindenburg when he was recalled to active duty and sent to stem the Russian invasion of East Prussia in August 1914. Partnered with Erich Ludendorff, Hindenburg became a powerful symbol of German military proficiency after impressive initial victories at Tannenberg and Masurian Lakes. Promoted to field marshal and given command of all German forces in the east, he led Germany from victory to victory as the western front stagnated. When stalemate and high losses at Verdun in 1916 discredited his main military rival and nominal superior, Erich von Falkenhayn, Hindenburg became chief of the imperial general staff with Ludendorff as his deputy, or first quartermaster general. Their partnership proved fatal for imperial Germany.

Wartime photographs showing a united triumvirate of the kaiser and his two warlords obscured friction and discord. Kaiser Wilhelm disliked Hindenburg and despised Ludendorff but did little to prevent them from forming a virtual military dictatorship after they successfully schemed to have Theobald von Bethmann Hollweg dismissed as chancellor in July 1917. The so-called Hindenburg Program to mobilize the German economy for total war strengthened the army temporarily at the price of permanently debilitating the home front. Against that backdrop Hindenburg oversaw Germany's fatal decision in January 1917 to resume the unrestricted submarine warfare that led to United States entry into the war in April; insisted on onerous demands (the short-lived Treaty of Brest-Litovsk) against a defeated Russia, which later spurred Entente demands at Versailles; and approved the Ludendorff Offensives from March to June 1918, a desperate gamble to destroy Entente forces before the American Expeditionary Forces (AEF) could arrive and deploy in large numbers, which ended in abdication and exile for the kaiser and exhaustion and collapse for imperial Germany.

Refusing to admit his own failings or culpability, Hindenburg in 1919 maliciously promoted the *Dolchstoßlegende,* or "stab-in-the-back myth," which blamed Bolsheviks, war profiteers, Jews, and other "November criminals" on the home front for the Second Reich's collapse. Marginalized at first, Hindenburg became in 1925 the calm eye in the cultural-political hurricane that was Weimar when he won election to the presidency. Dismissed as ponderous and inarticulate by young sophisticates, Hindenburg nevertheless embodied Prussian conservatism and mature male virility for millions of Germans. Like the postbellum American South with its enshrinement of Robert E. Lee, Weimar Germany needed a heroic and honorable paterfamilias to ease the pain of catastrophic and emasculating military defeat. Hindenburg became that symbol not only for the German right, but the center and much of the left as well. His reassuring solidity, devotion to duty, and quiet dignity paradoxically facilitated experiments in democracy.

Serving as *Reichspräsident* from 1925 until his death in 1934, the monarchist Hindenburg nevertheless remained hostile to Weimar's republican principles. As economic chaos polarized political discourse, Hindenburg turned reluctantly to the fascist NSDAP as offering the most promising alternative to maintaining order and military virtues while aggressively suppressing Bolshevik attempts at radical social experiments. It was a colossal blunder. His prestige did much to give the Nazi regime an initial leg up on its chief rivals. His death in 1934 freed Hitler and his henchmen to pursue unprecedented experiments in evil.

Paul von Hindenburg, our subtitle suggests, became the emblem and embodiment of German militarism. As a term, *militarism* is more descriptive than definitive. In its German contexts it involves a retrograde aspect, the continued influence of traditional military attitudes and considerations on modern sociopolitical systems. Militarism describes as well the permeation of military attitudes and values throughout German civil society and political culture. In both contexts Hindenburg was an iconic figure.

For encouraging us to write this biography and overseeing its publication, the authors wish to thank Paul M. Merzlak at Potomac Books, Inc. For reading previous versions of our manuscript, we wish to thank David S. Heidler, Holger H. Herwig, Michael S. Neiberg, Robert C. Pirro, and Gerhard L. Weinberg. For help with illustrations, we wish to acknowledge Duane Reed, archivist at the USAF Academy, as well as Donald Frazier for the maps. Finally, we wish to dedicate this book to Christine with love.

# Chronology

| | |
|---|---|
| *1847* | Born in Posen, Prussia (now Poznan, Poland), October 2. |
| *1859* | Attends cadets' academy at Wahlstatt in Liegnitz/Silesia. |
| *1863* | Transfers to Senior Cadet School in Berlin. |
| *1865* | Becomes lieutenant, Third Regiment of Foot Guards. |
| *1866* | Decorated for bravery, Battle of Königgrätz, Austro-Prussian War. |
| *1870* | Becomes battalion adjutant (later, regimental adjutant), Franco-Prussian War. |
| *1871* | Wilhelm I is crowned, Hall of Mirrors, Versailles, January 18. |
| *1873–1876* | Attends *Kriegsakademie*, Berlin. |
| *1877* | Appointed to general staff. |
| *1879* | Marries Gertrud Wilhelmine von Sperling. |
| *1885* | Appointed to imperial general staff. Serves with Alfred von Schlieffen. |
| *1889* | Joins War Ministry. |
| *1893* | Appointed commander, Ninety-first Infantry Regiment, Oldenburg. |
| *1896* | Appointed chief of staff, Eighth Army Corps, Coblenz. |
| *1900* | Appointed commander, Twenty-eighth Division, Karlsruhe. |
| *1905* | Appointed commander, Fourth Army Corps, Magdeburg. |

*1911*    Retires to Hanover, January 9.

*1914*    Recalled to active duty as commander, Eighth
         Army, August 22.
         Tannenberg, August 26–31; Masurian Lakes,
         September 9–14.
         Appointed supreme commander, German forces in
         the east, November 1.
         Promoted to field marshal, November 27.

*1915*    Second battle of Masurian Lakes is fought,
         February.
         Gorlice-Tarnów Offensive begins, May 2.
         Germans seize Warsaw, August 5.

*1916*    Verdun Offensive begins, February 21.
         Brusilov Offensive begins, June 4.
         Somme Offensive begins, July 1.
         Appointed chief of the general staff, August 29.
         Rumania collapses, December.
         Reichstag suggests peace negotiations, December.

*1917*    Unrestricted submarine warfare renewed,
         February 1.
         United States severs diplomatic relations,
         February 3.
         Troops withdraw to the Hindenburg Line,
         February to April.
         Zimmermann telegram, February 28.
         United States declares war on Germany, April 6.
         Bethmann Hollweg forced out as chancellor, July 4
         Reichstag Peace Resolution is passed, July 19.
         Communist revolution takes place in Russia,
         October.
         Armistice is signed between Germany and Russia,
         December 15.

*1918*    Woodrow Wilson announces the Fourteen Points,
         January 8.

Treaty of Brest-Litovsk is signed, March 3.
Ludendorff Offensives take place, March 21 to
July 18.
Entente counteroffensive begins, July 18.
"Black Day of the German Army" takes place,
Amiens, August 8.
Ludendorff tells the kaiser the war must end,
August 13.
Prince Max von Baden forms new government,
September 28.
Germany requests armistice, October 4.
Ludendorff resigns, October 26; kaiser refuses
Hindenburg's resignation.
Mutiny of *Kriegsmarine* at Kiel, November 4.
German Republic declared, November 9; kaiser
abdicates.
Armistice is signed at Compiègne, November 11.

*1919*    Treaty of Versailles is signed, June 28.
Hindenburg retires, July 4.
Reichstag testimony supports *Dolchstoßlegende*,
November 18.

*1923*    French and Belgian forces occupy the Ruhr;
Germany devalues mark, triggering runaway
inflation, January.
Munich Putsch effected by Hitler and Ludendorff,
November 8.

*1925*    Elected *Reichspräsident* of Weimar, April 26.

*1929*    Great Depression begins, October 29.

*1930*    Chancellor Heinrich Brüning dissolves Reichstag,
July.

*1932*    Defeats Hitler for presidency, April 10.

*1933*    Appoints Hitler chancellor, January 30.
Reichstag fire takes place, February 27.

*1934*    "Night of the Long Knives" takes place, June 30.

Dies at Neudeck (now Podzamek, Poland), August
2; Hitler merges offices of president and chancellor,
taking title of *der Führer* (leader).

Interred at the Tannenberg Memorial, August 6.

*1945*   Hindenburg's coffin removed from Tannenberg;
Germans destroy the monument to prevent its
capture, January.

*1946*   Hindenburg's coffin and regimental colors
reinterred at *Elisabethkirche*, Marburg an der Lahn,
August.

# HINDENBURG

# Prewar

Paul Ludwig Hans Anton von Beneckendorff und von Hindenburg was born on October 2, 1847, in Posen, West Prussia. As a *Junker,* a member of Prussia's East Elbian aristocracy, and his family's eldest son, he was expected to serve in the officer corps. Young Hindenburg willingly embraced that destiny. The Beneckendorff side of his family traced its lineage back to the crusading Teutonic knights of the medieval period and was especially proud of its deep roots in Brandenburg. The Hindenburg side was of more recent origin, but the great Frederick himself had granted an estate at Neudeck to an ancestor, Colonel Otto Frederick von Hindenburg, who lost a leg in the king's service at the battle of Torgau in 1760.

As a child, Hindenburg thrived on stories of heroic battlefield deeds told by an aged gardener on the family estate who had served as a drummer boy under Frederick the Great. His grandfather further regaled the young boy with stories of Napoleon Bonaparte. Hindenburg never questioned his calling as a Prussian officer, first fighting for the king of Prussia, then serving the kaiser and a new German empire. By his own admission, "It does not matter to what part of our German Fatherland my profession has called me, I have always felt myself an 'Old Prussian.'"[1]

For someone with a military calling, Prussia in the 1850s and 1860s was an opportune place and time to live. Having recovered from humiliating defeat at Napoleon's hands in 1806 to play a crucial role in his defeat in 1815, Prussia at midcentury sought to consolidate and extend its influence in Germany. The challenge for a state with limited resources was to avoid fighting long wars, especially on two fronts. The eventual solution involved combining diplomatic acumen with military proficiency. In Otto von Bismarck (1815–1898), Prussia discovered a master conductor of the concert of Europe and a skillful practitioner of *Realpolitik*. Recognizing both the inherent strategic vulnerabilities and opportunities of Prussia's central position in Europe, Bismarck moved cautiously and craftily to redraw the continent's map to Prussia's advantage. And in Helmuth von Moltke, chief of the general staff from 1857 to 1890, Prussia possessed a master of total war waged for limited objectives.

Hindenburg's *Junker* heritage made it possible for him to play a central role in realizing Prussian ambitions. His father, a reserve infantry officer, taught his eldest son geography and history. His mother, whom Hindenburg worshiped, inspired in him a simple yet resilient faith in a stern, Protestant god. Strict they were, but Hindenburg's parents merely echoed a prevailing Prussian code of discipline, duty, and obedience to higher authority. Even the young Hindenburg's nurse was known to bark, "Silence in the ranks!" to squelch childish complaints. Confronting adults, Hindenburg and his siblings were expected to snap to attention in heel-clicking unison. Strict family discipline was sound preparation for Spartan years to come.

In these impressionable years, the youthful Hindenburg traveled with his parents from garrison town to garrison town. Barracks, shouted commands, and goose-stepping soldiers formed the backdrop to his life. Immersed in the soldierly activities and values that characterized a proud and resurgent Prussia, Hindenburg reveled in the prospect of adding his name to the roll of Prussia's military worthies.

In 1859 the not-quite-twelve-year-old Hindenburg prepared to enter the Prussian Cadet Corps. Before he did, he soberly composed his last will and testament, leaving his prized possessions to his siblings. At Wahlstatt in Liegnitz, Silesia, young Hindenburg shed tears as he bade farewell to his father, but he quickly wiped them away and mingled among his fellow cadets. Their barracks overlooked the battlefield of the Katzbach, where Marshal Blücher had dealt French forces a setback in 1813 that helped to frustrate Napoleon's victory at Dresden. Hindenburg admired the redoubtable "Papa Blücher" throughout his life, hanging his portrait above his writing table. Later, many would compare Hindenburg's partnership with Erich Ludendorff to the aging Blücher's relationship to his younger and brilliant chief of staff, August von Gneisenau.

A revealing portrait of Cadet Hindenburg's martial preferences emerged in designs he sketched for a display in his wardrobe. "At the rear," he enthused to his parents, he would place

> a big Prussian eagle on the wall; in the center, on an elevation, 'Old Fritz' and his generals; at the foot of the elevation a number of Black Hussars; in front a chain with cannon posted behind it, more in the foreground two watchman's booths, with two grenadiers of the time of Frederick the Great.[2]

His literary interests, such as they were, were confined to action and adventure stories, with James Fenimore Cooper's *Pathfinder* making its way onto a Christmas list he sent to his parents.

In enduring the harsh regimen of cadet life, young Hindenburg demonstrated moral uprightness and physical hardiness without showing any particular intellectual qualities. Fellow cadets remembered him as a stickler for detail and a trifle lacking in humor, yet also as evenhanded and compassionate. Hindenburg had his own fond memories of these days. Reminiscing in a letter to the headmaster at Wahlstatt, he humbly attributed his

own success during World War I to the school's "severe educa-
tion," which inculcated self-discipline and "manly strength and
a feeling of comradeship which has always accompanied me
throughout my life."[3]

That package combined with his *Junker* heritage earned Hindenburg a transfer in 1863 to the prestigious Senior Cadet School
in Berlin, a standard preliminary to a commission in the elite
Prussian Guard. Too young to serve in the brief Prusso-Danish
War of 1864, Hindenburg instead served as page to the widowed
Queen Elizabeth of Prussia. Her gift of a pocket watch he kept
on his person for the remainder of his days. After passing his ex-
aminations, he was commissioned a second lieutenant in the
Third Regiment of the Foot Guards on April 7, 1865.

Eager to prove himself in battle, the new lieutenant did not
have long to wait. In 1866 Austria and Prussia settled by combat
that which they could not decide by diplomacy: which Germanic state was to control the fate of central Europe. In the Austro-Prussian, or Seven Weeks', War of 1866, Prussia reaped the
dividends of comprehensive military reforms undertaken earlier
in the decade. Under Moltke, the Prussian army stressed speed
of mobilization and strategic mobility based on railroads and
telegraph lines.[4] Moltke also succeeded in strengthening military
proficiency through painstaking staff work and realistic training.
Better organized, led, and equipped, Prussia nevertheless faced a
formidable Austrian army whose full strength was divided by the
need to conduct major campaigns in Italy as well as Austria
proper.

The key battle was at Königgrätz on July 3, 1866. "I rejoice in
this bright-colored future," Hindenburg wrote to his parents
prior to the battle. "For the soldier war is the normal state of
things. . . . If I fall it is the most honorable and beautiful death."[5]
That July day found Hindenburg commanding a platoon on the
skirmish line during the guard's crucial attack on the heights of
Chlum. It was high time a Hindenburg again smelled powder
and tasted victory on the battlefield, he later wrote, and he ac-
quitted himself with energy and valor. Under fire from Austrian

artillery, Hindenburg rushed the position. A case-shot round perforated the eagle on his helmet, grazing his head and momentarily disorienting him. After realizing his wound was minor, Hindenburg continued the charge, participating with his company in the capture of several guns. Later he was in the thick of bitter hand-to-hand fighting for the key village of Rosberitz. Superior morale and willingness to seize the initiative, enhanced by better weaponry, carried the day in his sector, Hindenburg concluded. The damaged helmet became a lifelong memento to him of his glory days leading from the front.

At the victory parade in Berlin, Hindenburg received from his commander the Order of the Red Eagle, Fourth Class, with Swords. An elderly lady stepped forward with a pin so that the young lieutenant could properly display his badge of courage. Hindenburg never forgot the date or place where he received his first decoration for gallantry. Upon being promoted to field marshal in 1914, an old comrade of Königgrätz wrote to congratulate him. Thanking him for his kind words, Hindenburg included a money order with his reply, asking his comrade to "spend this sum in drinking a toast to the health of our most gracious Kaiser and King and to our dear old regiment."[6]

After settling accounts with Austria, Bismarck and Moltke realized that the ambitions of Napoleon III of France needed curbing if Prussia was to dominate *Mitteleuropa*. As Bismarck worked to maneuver France into conceding German unification, whether in the council chamber or on the battlefield, Hindenburg assumed duties as a battalion adjutant and hoped for another short, victorious war. When Napoleon III impetuously declared war on Prussia on July 19, 1870, Hindenburg once again found himself in the thick of the action—and once again his luck held. His battalion took heavy casualties during the storming of St. Privat in front of Metz, but only his boot was struck by a round from a *mitrailleuse* (an early machine gun). Otherwise, Hindenburg emerged unscathed from the intense fighting, a fate he attributed to providence. He later memorialized the soldiers' sacrifice at St. Privat, writing that "spiritual enthusiasm, a stern resolve to conquer, and the holy lust of battle" drove the men forward against sleeting French fire. Having earned the Iron Cross, Second Class, for this glorious moment, he continued throughout his life to favor "stout-hearted action" and "strength of character" over "the refinements of intellect" in the prosecution of war.[7]

Upon the promotion of his commander to colonel, Hindenburg followed him upward and became regimental adjutant of the Third Foot Guards. After Napoleon III's surrender at Sedan failed to end the war, Prussian-led forces settled down to a lengthy siege of Paris. Many German soldiers from Moltke downwards deplored French stubbornness in prolonging the war, but not Hindenburg. He wrote that republican resistance had preserved the military honor of France. He especially praised the republic's ruthless postwar suppression of the Paris Commune. Most memorably for Lieutenant von Hindenburg, his regiment elected him to represent them at the proclamation of Wilhelm I as Kaiser, or emperor, of the Second Reich in the Hall of Mirrors, Versailles, on January 18, 1871. Six weeks later, he rode at the head of a regiment of Hussars through the Arc de Triomphe in Paris, then paraded before the kaiser at Longchamps. Remaining with the army of occupation, Hindenburg eventually returned to Germany in June, this time parading through the Brandenburg Gate in Berlin.

Photographs of Hindenburg from this period show a strapping, confident officer, his cap or helmet cocked at a jaunty angle. Well over six feet tall, the adult Hindenburg was sturdily built, with wide shoulders, thick neck, and prominent jaw. His steely visage was softened by calm blue-gray eyes known more for appraising glances than intimidating glares. Only later did he become the bulky and stentorian field marshal of history, with bristling crew cut and thrusting mustache. Even then he enjoyed the constitution of an ox, never suffering a serious illness until his decline in the late 1920s due to old age.

But dotage remained in the distant future. As a young man Hindenburg had helped to establish the Second Reich, an event that marked a watershed in European history. Seeking to distinguish himself in battle and to restore luster to his family name, he had accomplished both. With some satisfaction he settled down to a steady if unspectacular rise through the army's ranks.

Imperial Germany's rise fundamentally upset the balance of power in Europe. Since the Thirty Years' War in the seventeenth century, the German states had remained fragmented, with Prussia at best the weakest of the European Big Five (the other four being France, Britain, Russia, and Austria). Suddenly, Germany was militarily Europe's most dynamic nation-state. As it continued to industrialize, the "restless Reich" surged ever ahead.

A newcomer to European imperialism, Germany under Bismarck's steady hand pursued an assertive, yet sober, foreign policy, which included an alliance in 1879 with the dual monarchy of Austria-Hungary and attempts at rapprochement with tsarist Russia. Domestic politics included a bitterly contested *Kulturkampf*, or struggle for cultural authority between Bismarck and Pius IX and the Roman Catholic Church. With the accession in 1888 of Wilhelm II to the imperial throne, German foreign policy soon entered a more bellicose phase after the new kaiser dispensed with Bismarck in 1890.

High-level political machinations and cultural struggles were far removed from Hindenburg's insular military world. After attending the *Kriegsakademie* (War Academy) in Berlin from 1873 to 1876, he was appointed to the general staff and promoted to captain in 1878. The next year he married a general's daughter, Gertrud Wilhelmine von Sperling (1860–1921), who was thirteen years his junior. They enjoyed a long and happy marriage blessed with three children, a son and two daughters. Hindenburg raised his son, Oskar, to follow in his footsteps, often addressing him as *Herr Leutnant*. Oskar later became an officer and played an influential role in shaping his father's course of action as president of the Weimar Republic.

Promotions in peacetime came regularly if not rapidly. Reassigned in 1885 to the imperial general staff, Hindenburg, now a major, served under Count Alfred Graf von Schlieffen. He focused on Russian tactics in the east and how outnumbered German forces might aggressively counter a multipronged Russian invasion of East Prussia—studies that served him well at Tannenberg in 1914. Tightlipped with his praise, the laconic Schlieffen awarded Hindenburg high marks when he concluded, "I consider him capable of conducting operations."[8] So he would prove to be.

The death of Wilhelm I in 1888 deeply saddened the committed monarchist. Hindenburg had the honor of participating in the vigil to the kaiser, during which he hoisted his five-year-old Oskar for a better view and whispered, "If you never forget this moment as long as you live you will always do right." One wonders if Hindenburg was also speaking inwardly to himself. Requisitioning a block of gray marble from the cathedral floor upon which the kaiser's coffin had rested, Hindenburg kept it on his desk thereafter, writing "I need not attempt to clothe in words the thoughts which rise within me, even today [1919], when I look at that piece of stone."[9]

After Wilhelm II dispensed with Bismarck's services in 1890, imperial Germany embarked on a foreign policy defined by a quest for *Weltpolitik* (world power). Meanwhile, Hindenburg toiled in the War Ministry, overseeing tedious revisions to field-engineering regulations. He did not chaff at this inglorious task. Rather, he saw it as another opportunity to serve. Willing to do routine assignments and to do them well, his professionalism earned Hindenburg the thanks of his superiors, if not always high praise.

Hindenburg's favorite tour of duty came when he assumed command in 1893 of the Ninety-first Infantry Regiment at Oldenburg. A regimental commander, he later wrote, should seek to stamp his personality on his unit. Hindenburg's philosophy was "to cultivate a sense of chivalry among my officers, and efficiency and firm discipline" within his battalions, as well as "the love of work and independence side by side with a high ideal of service." As a regimental colonel, Hindenburg worked his men hard but also cared for their needs, earning their respect and affection.

While seeking to instill unit pride and uphold discipline, there was nothing of the strutting martinet about him. On the occasion of Hindenburg's seventieth birthday in 1917, the kaiser granted him the singular honor of permanent attachment to his old regiment, a distinction Hindenburg cherished for the remainder of his life.[10]

While a regimental commander, Hindenburg celebrated in 1896 the twenty-fifth anniversary of the founding of the Second Reich. Speaking soldier to soldier, he told his regiment how Germany "arose amid the thunder of guns. And soldiers' courage and soldiers' faith shall also protect and defend it, should any dare to lay hands upon this precious jewel, for which streams of soldiers' blood have been shed."[11] Twenty-five years of peace had served only to stoke the embers of Hindenburg's military ardor.

That same year Hindenburg reluctantly left his regiment when he became chief of staff of the Eighth Army Corps in Coblenz. Promoted to brigadier general in 1897, he served with efficiency until earning a divisional command in 1900. He served as major general and commander of the Twenty-eighth Infantry Division at Karlsruhe until 1905, when he reached the pinnacle of his peacetime military career as *General der Infanterie* (lieutenant general) and commander, Fourth Army Corps, at Magdeburg. For more than eight years he served as one of only twenty-four corps commanders in Germany.

Although considered for higher posts, including that of chief of the imperial general staff on Schlieffen's retirement, Hindenburg remained in place. Rumor had it that in 1908, during one of Wilhelm II's much ballyhooed *Kaisermanöver* (field exercises), Hindenburg's career suffered a setback when he unwisely allowed the dilettantish and petulant kaiser to lose. Although Hindenburg later denied this rumor, he was not one of the kaiser's favorites; the insecure and testy Wilhelm preferred officers with greater panache. His career stuck in neutral, Hindenburg retired to Hanover in January 1911. Going on sixty-four, he wrote that it was time to make room for younger men. His military career had reached a respectable, if unremarkable, end, or so it seemed. If one includes his cadet years, he had served Prussia and Germany with distinction for better than half a century.

At first, retirement seemed agreeable. An avid hunter, Hindenburg amassed trophies and bagged game at rates even Theodore Roosevelt may have found difficult to match.[12] He expressed a long-submerged sentimental and devotional side by collecting Madonna-and-child images and paintings, showing more enthusiasm than taste in his acquisitions. Meanwhile, he fostered Oskar's military career while marrying his two daughters off to *Junkers*. Yet, it was also apparent that he missed serving kaiser and country. Although without any assignment in the mobilized army, Hindenburg held himself ready as war increasingly seemed likely, keeping both physically fit and professionally alert.

Hindenburg's mature views on society and war might briefly be summarized as follows. He expressed absolute faith in the army, asking rhetorically, "Where have the idea of equality and the sense of unity among our people found more striking expression than in the all-leveling school of our great national army?" In the same vein, he continued,

> The conviction that the subordination of the individual to the good of the community was not only a necessity, but a positive blessing, had gripped the mind of the German army, and through it that of the German nation. It was only thus that the colossal feats were possible which were needed, and which we performed under the stress of dire necessity and against a world of enemies.[13]

Written in 1919, this revealing statement reflected a self-fulfilling vision shared by many prominent German military men. Prior to 1914, they saw their country as being in a state of *Einkreisung*, surrounded by enemies, hemmed in and oppressed. That attitude often provoked aggressive, even bellicose, responses that encouraged rivals to become enemies instead of partners. Yet, the mind-set was not unique to Germany. Throughout Europe war was considered the ultimate test both of individual masculinity and national fitness, consistent with a biological imperative summed up in the catchphrase "survival of the fittest" and a marked preference for settling differences on the field of battle—at least in principle.

Few German officers appear to have read Carl von Clause-witz's *Vom Krieg* (*On War*). Those who did read it so selectively that *Vom Krieg* was known misleadingly as the "Bible of König-grätz." Ignored or misunderstood was Clausewitz's dialectical philosophy of war as a continuation of politics. Ultimately, German officers like Hindenburg believed wars were prosecuted best through battles of annihilation, with *Geist,* or patriotic spirit, providing the winning edge.[14] Recalling the Franco-Prussian War, Hindenburg noted that the French had had better rifles, but the Prussians possessed the intangibles of superior moral energy and will to prevail. The Second Reich, forged with blood and iron, was to be tempered through selfless action manifested in the motto *Ich dien* (I serve), superior military skill, and inculcation of a war-winning spirit.

Patriotic commitment and tactical excellence carried Germany a long way in World War I, but reflected as well the narrowness of approach shared by Hindenburg, Ludendorff, and their peers. They were *Fachmenschen,* or specialists, technically astute, loyal to a fault, but confined to an operational and Eurocentric perspective that eschewed study and reflection about the wider socioeconomic and political aspects of war. Hindenburg's military career took him to Austria, France, and Russia, and he once visited Italy; otherwise, he spent his entire life in Germany. Lacking firsthand knowledge of the world outside of Europe, or of the world of business and industry within and without Europe, Hindenburg also had little exposure to military grand strategy. Lacking mental dexterity, he preferred to confront the challenge of solving difficult operational problems by fostering tactical excellence and an aggressive spirit.

For Hindenburg, war was a craft to be mastered, not a dialectic to be parsed and synthesized. Better to impose one's will on the enemy—to be the hunter and not the hunted—than to relinquish the initiative.[15] Such an aggressive approach served him well on the eastern front in 1914. That was not always the case in a great war of unparalleled dimensions that brought Hindenburg from oblivion to the pinnacle of power.

# The Eastern Front, 1914–1916

"FIRST WEIGH the cost and then dare," Hindenburg once declared.[1] Many leaders weighed the costs of war in 1914 and decided they were worth daring. Indeed, war came to Europe in 1914 because nations were mentally prepared for it. Militarism was widespread, particularly in Germany where the historian and social Darwinist Heinrich von Treitschke wrote of war's grandeur, its "utter annihilation of puny man in the great conception of the state."[2] General Friedrich von Bernhardi, in *Deutschland und der nächste Krieg* (*Germany and the Next War*, 1912), called war "not merely a necessary element in the life of nations, but an indispensable factor of culture, in which a true civilized nation finds the highest expression of strength and vitality." Popular catchphrases such as *Am deutschen Wesen wird die Welt genesen* (Germanness will cure the world) captured a pervasive chauvinistic nationalism. Anticipating *der frischfröhliche Krieg*, a fresh and joyful war, young patriotic Germans answered the call to arms in 1914 with pride and celerity.

Yet, if "give war a chance" was the chant of many Germans, others feared the potential havoc that a prolonged war would unleash. Chancellor Theobald von Bethmann Hollweg spoke of a "leap in the dark" that "would topple many a throne," including quite possibly the kaiser's. Unease at the high-stakes military gamble Germany was embarking upon led to pessimism. Enthusiastic bursts of patriotism served to suppress doubt, but they left behind a residue of unease. Seductive visions of victory through glorious battles of annihilation reinforced insouciance and, in retrospect, a misplaced belief in generals' ability to control war. Suppressed for the moment were the German general staff's own concerns that the Schlieffen Plan was balanced on a knife's edge. Instead of rapid victory, war by railroad timetable might end in a multitrack train wreck.[3]

Other countries shared this unease, including Britain. Rudyard Kipling's "For All We Have and Are," which appeared in the London *Times* on September 2, 1914, expressed both the hazards of war and the necessity of keeping upper lips stiff in confronting German militarism:

> Once more we hear the word
> That sickened earth of old:
> "No law except the sword
> Unsheathed and uncontrolled."
> Once more it knits mankind,
> Once more the nations go
> To meet and break and bind
> A crazed and driven foe.

Fully expecting a short war, Hindenburg paced restlessly in Hanover as seven German armies swept into France, Luxembourg, and Belgium in August. As the Schlieffen Plan unfolded in the west, Russia mobilized weeks earlier than predicted and in mid-August invaded East Prussia with two armies. The cry of *Kossaken kommen!* sent tens of thousands of villagers onto the roads, no matter that the Russian army's actual Cossacks were on the whole thoroughly domesticated: often no more than farm boys mounted on plow horses, with officers who wore glasses and sported paunches.[4] Nevertheless, the image of savages who raped, killed, and plundered at will was strong enough that even officers groveled for their lives when they fell into Cossack hands.

Streams of German refugees reached near flood tide when the Russian First Army, the northern arm of the invasion's pincers, administered a sharp local defeat to the Germans at Gumbinnen on August 20. When the German Eighth Army's commanding general and his chief of staff suggested a general withdrawal to the west bank of the Vistula, a panicky Moltke the Younger sacked them. Moltke and the *Oberste Heeresleitung* (OHL, or Army High Command) then had to select a new command team to stabilize Germany's eastern front.

Moltke's selection of Erich Ludendorff as the new chief of staff of the Eighth Army was easily made. Ludendorff had overseen the general staff's prewar blueprint for mobilization until outspoken advocacy of army expansion landed him in political hot water. Exiled to a socially second-rate regimental command in the industrial city of Düsseldorf, when war came he distinguished himself within days. Attached as deputy chief of staff to the Second Army, Ludendorff assumed command of a leaderless brigade, stormed the Belgian fortress of Liège, and boldly demanded its surrender by hammering on the citadel's door with the hilt of his sword. For this act the kaiser decorated the "hero of Liège" with the *Pour le Mérite* (the coveted Blue Max). Audacious and technically brilliant though Ludendorff was, he was known to be a hothead; he suffered from nerves when plans went awry; and his social origins were not quite top-drawer. Ludendorff would make an excellent chief of staff, Moltke concluded, but someone higher ranking was needed to take command and provide stability and aristocratic presence.

As Moltke debated the choice, a distant relative of Hindenburg attached to OHL recalled that Hindenburg stood ready in Hanover, conveniently centered on a major rail line. The telegram went forth, the retired general replied "Ready," and a special two-car train carrying Ludendorff from Coblenz made a stopover at Hanover in the early morning hours of August 23. Lacking a regulation field gray uniform, Hindenburg improvised with black trousers and a peacetime Prussian blue tunic let out by his wife to accommodate a postretirement paunch. Ludendorff stepped forward, saluted his oddly garbed commander, and stood respectfully aside as the newly promoted *Generaloberst* (colonel general) bid adieu to his wife. Together Hindenburg and Ludendorff readied themselves for the journey to East Prussia. It was their first meeting and the beginning of a remarkable strategic partnership.

Hindenburg's new chief of staff was born on April 9, 1865, two days after Hindenburg had been commissioned a second lieutenant. Son of a bourgeois father and an aristocratic mother, Ludendorff reflected the new wave of general staff officers distinguished more by military proficiency than by aristocratic lineage. He was, in Basil Liddell Hart's telling phrase, a "robot Napoleon." He had Napoleon's work ethic, endurance, and capacious mind, but none of his charisma or inspirational qualities. Peering through a monocle, a sternly self-important expression animating a bulky and somewhat flaccid frame, Ludendorff in peacetime had moved expertly from crisis to crisis. Irascible, humorless, indefatigable, he was the stereotype of a Prussian officer. His main flaw was unbridled ambition. Subordinates respected him but feared his sarcastic tongue and dictatorial ways. In his unrefined bossiness and mastery of minutiae, he was the antithesis of what the kaiser looked for in his senior officers (*der Feldwebel*, or that sergeant major, the kaiser was heard to call him), but no one else in August 1914 had Ludendorff's combination of tactical skill, operational insight, and boundless energy.

On the train Ludendorff summarized the military situation in East Prussia. After half an hour, Hindenburg nodded his agreement and then set the standard for their relationship by calmly going to sleep. As Hindenburg explained in his memoirs, there was little they could do until they reached Eighth Army headquarters at Marienburg. Hindenburg's calm confidence reassured the excitable Ludendorff. Already these men had begun to form a symbiotic relationship.

In their postwar memoirs, both men celebrated the Hegelian synthesis they had forged during the war. Ludendorff gushed that he and the field marshal had worked together "like one man, in the most perfect harmony." Hindenburg's account was more measured and telling. He described their bond as a "happy marriage" in which they became "one in thought and action." More to the point, Hindenburg admitted that he gave "free scope to the intellectual powers, the almost superhuman capacity for work and untiring resolution" of his "brother warrior."[5] That last phrase suggests the most appropriate trope for their relationship. Hindenburg was like an older, shrewder, but less gifted, brother who, as the war progressed, found himself eclipsed by the unbounded ambition of a younger sibling.

At first the older comrade provided much needed stiffening to the younger. Recalled to active duty at the age of sixty-seven, Hindenburg had little left to prove. Having already served with distinction during the German wars of unification, he only wanted to be of service for a week, a month, or however long it took Germany to win this war. Having assiduously studied the geography of East Prussia and having been committed since the 1890s to the idea of repulsing a Russian offensive with aggressive counterattacks, he quickly grasped and approved Ludendorff's concepts for redeploying the Eighth Army.

Arriving at Eighth Army headquarters in the late afternoon, Hindenburg's commanding physical presence and emotional imperturbability proved a tonic. Few commanders possessed the force of will to steady not only an inexperienced army whose previous commander and chief of staff had been summarily cashiered, but also a skillful but anxious chief of staff whose imagination plagued him with paralyzing visions of catastrophic defeat and failure. Teaming with Lieutenant Colonel (later General) Max Hoffmann, a highly capable and equally arrogant officer of the army staff, Hindenburg and Ludendorff confirmed plans to concentrate Eighth Army's strength against the Russians advancing from the south.

Facilitated by the Russians' failure to follow up their victory at

Gumbinnen, the Germans took advantage of their road and railroad networks to bring the equivalent of five army corps against a Russian Second Army suffering from overextension and disrupted communications. On August 27, First Corps crushed the Russian left wing. Two more corps, reaching their positions by hard marching in the brutal August heat, drove in the Russian right. The Russian commander sought to restore the situation by attacking forward with the five divisions of his center and came closer to success than is generally realized. By the evening of August 28, however, German forces advancing on the flanks had closed an unbreakable circle around the Russians.[6]

Victory, the saying goes, has many fathers, but defeat is an orphan. After the fact, many self-proclaimed "victors of Tannenberg" stepped forward. But as Hindenburg himself noted, only he would have taken the blame if the battle had gone the other way. Tannenberg was Hindenburg's victory. He knew what to do and, more importantly, what not to do. By restoring calm at headquarters, he created an environment in which officers could get on with their jobs. Meddling or micromanaging was simply not his way. Instead, he provided the force of command by holding his nerve and calling Russia's bluff. An overly ambitious Russian advance, launched prematurely to aid France, was almost fated to fail if German forces moved expeditiously to outflank and outmaneuver their less mobile Russian counterparts.

Tannenberg was nevertheless a stunning victory. It marked the destruction of the Russian Second Army, the suicide of its commander, and the capture of ninety-two thousand men and nearly four hundred guns. Yet, it did not even come near to driving Russia from the war—Schlieffen's criterion for decisive victory. In this it was ironically similar to the Carthaginian victory at Cannae, which only reconfirmed Rome's determination to resist. Tannenberg's legacies were nonetheless important. Together with the victory over the Russian First Army at Masurian Lakes in September, it reinvigorated a German war effort seeking to cope with a conflict of unexpected length and dimensions. Even more importantly, Tannenberg created a new national hero.

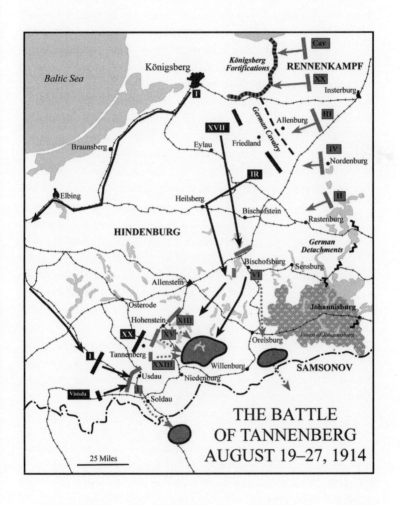

THE BATTLE
OF TANNENBERG
AUGUST 19–27, 1914

From retirement and obscurity, Paul von Beneckendorff (he was still listed under "B" in the retirement roll) emerged reborn as Paul von Hindenburg, savior of the fatherland. A battle cruiser was commissioned in his newly minted name. Posen opened a museum in his honor. Even the town of Zabrze in Silesia adopted Hindenburg's name as its own.

It was Hindenburg, the hero of the hour, who suggested naming the battle "Tannenberg" to avenge a defeat in 1410 suffered by the Teutonic knights at the hands of Polish and Lithuanian forces.[7] Other villages were closer to the center of the battle, but none had names that resonated. An army marches as much on its myths as its stomach. Tannenberg not only became a smashing victory over the Russians; it also redeemed the sacrifice of the Teutonic knights of old. Thus did Hindenburg transform victory into myth—a quasi-religious deliverance.

His memoirs took up the theme. After the battle Hindenburg wrote,

> I entered the church, close by the old castle of the Teutonic knights, while divine service was being held. As the clergyman uttered his closing words all those present, young soldiers as well as elderly *Landsturm,* sank to their knees under the overwhelming impression of their experiences. It was a worthy curtain to their heroic achievements.[8]

During the war Hindenburg boasted that "the battlefield where the Teutonic knights were defeated was the size of my nail. But the battlefield on which I defeated the Slavs is as large as my hand. It is a great joy to me that I was able to wipe out that disgrace."[9]

Awarded the *Pour le Mérite* for Tannenberg (on this occasion Ludendorff settled for the Iron Cross, Second Class), Hindenburg demonstrated a modern sense of public relations. He cultivated a persona, combining granite-hard authority and grandfatherly geniality, which won the approval of millions of ordinary Germans searching for a hero to inspire them in an increasingly difficult war. Unlike the kaiser, who found himself a spectator to a war he helped to create, Hindenburg became a public icon and popular hero. Wooden statues of him (known as *Nagelsäulen*) soon sprouted in cities and towns throughout Germany. The largest one, a twenty-eight-ton behemoth in the Königsplatz next to the Reichstag, was raised to mark the first anniversary of Tannenberg in August 1915. Germans supported the war effort by buying nails to pound into the statues, a ritual that Albert Speer, later Hitler's architect, recalled participating in as a young boy.[10] The banalities of Hindenburg's table talk passed for the wisdom of Germany's collective soul.

The worst excesses of the cult of Hindenburg, however, lay in the future. As Ludendorff redeployed the Eighth Army to maul and force the retreat of the Russian First Army at Masurian Lakes, thereby liberating East Prussia, the Schlieffen Plan collapsed in France along with its implementer, Moltke. To fill Moltke's shoes, the kaiser chose the Prussian war minister, Erich von Falkenhayn. Falkenhayn faced the daunting challenge of fighting a land war in France and Russia while waging a war at sea with Great Britain. He was not helped by the fact that the general staff and OHL lacked a contingency plan in case the Schlieffen Plan failed. Thus, there was no consensus about what to do next. Falkenhayn and the OHL had to improvise under pressure.[11]

Predictably, Hindenburg and Ludendorff argued for the east as the decisive theater. Besides victories at Tannenberg and Masurian Lakes, they could point to the creation of the Ninth Army from forces already in the theater, and its successful deployment into Poland to rescue Austro-Hungarian forces on the verge of collapse. Yet, in Falkenhayn's view, "The East gives nothing back."[12] He meant that Russian forces could refuse to give battle and instead conduct a strategic withdrawal, scorching the earth as they went—the same strategy that in 1812 compelled Napoleon's disastrous retreat from Moscow.

Denying Hindenburg and Ludendorff's request for reinforcements to attempt a huge encirclement of Russian forces in Poland, Falkenhayn instead looked to the western front for rapid decision. Seeking to turn the left flank of the Entente line, he was frustrated in October and November 1914 in bloody encounter battles around Ypres in Belgium. The images accompanying these battles of young and enthusiastic volunteers mowed down by the thousands (the notorious *Kindermord bei Ypern,* or massacre of the innocents) as they sang *Deutschland über Alles* (Germany above all) did much to discredit Falkenhayn. The operational result was no more positive than the moral: a four-hundred-mile line of rudimentary trenches stretching from the English Channel to the Swiss border. Strengthened by machine guns, wire, and artillery, the trench system produced gridlock. Not until the spring of 1918 did the western front move more than ten miles east or west due to enemy action.

Falkenhayn's gamble in the west had failed, yet he retained the kaiser's ear. Handsome, diplomatic, and polished, Falkenhayn cut an impressive figure. Well educated and proficient in several languages, he was, in the kaiser's eyes, the embodiment of *Junker* distinction. Personalities matter in war, where moral factors are so important. An insecure and image-conscious kaiser felt much more comfortable conversing with the courtly and deferential Falkenhayn than with the gruff and taciturn Hindenburg and his Golem-like alter ego, Ludendorff. Until mid-1916, Falkenhayn provided overall direction to Germany's strategy.

In the first few months of Falkenhayn's service as chief of the general staff, Hindenburg and Ludendorff could do little but clamor for more men and matériel to be sent eastwards. Once Germany had committed nearly seven eighths of its army to force a decision in the west, it was too much to expect, psychologically and logistically, for Falkenhayn and the OHL to do a complete about-face and seek decisive victory in the east. Paris seemed enticingly close, much closer than Moscow. Memories of glorious victories in the Franco-Prussian War lingered long and died hard. In retrospect, however, Falkenhayn reinforced failure. The prospect of defeating Russia in 1914 was a long shot. Yet, seeking decision in the west without the benefit of surprise—in a symmetrical battle of near equals—was the strategic equivalent of trying to win a head-butting contest against a brick wall.

Compared to bloody attrition and stalemate in the west, the east continued to produce tactical victories for Germany, if not for its ally Austria-Hungary. Indeed, a major flaw in Germany's war effort was a consistent failure to coordinate strategy with Austria-Hungary. In the early weeks of the war, Franz Conrad von Hötzendorf, chief of the Austro-Hungarian general staff, split his forces with the intention of punishing Serbia while simultaneously advancing against Russia. In a series of vicious encounter battles in August and September, five Russian armies in Galicia overwhelmed outnumbered Austrian forces, sending them reeling backwards.

Incredibly, Austria-Hungary and Germany had each expected the other to launch a major offensive against Russia. As a result, while German forces hung on by their fingernails in East Prussia, Austro-Hungarian forces were being crushed in isolation around Lemberg and points south. They suffered crippling casualties: a quarter of a million killed and wounded, with another hundred thousand captured. Even worse, the Austrian army lost its core of veteran commissioned and noncommissioned officers, who provided the nervous system for a multiethnic army.

Grievous Austrian losses generated little sympathy in Germany. A typical critique flowed from Hindenburg's pen. Hapsburg leaders had failed to devote adequate resources for war, Hindenburg wrote, and their soldiers paid the price. Ludendorff in 1915 wrote of military "incompetence," referred to Austrians as "this miserable people," and complained that Germany was "shackled to a corpse." On the other side of the fence, Conrad's attitude might best be summed up by his description of Germany as "the secret enemy."[13] An increasing number of senior Hapsburg officers and officials shared this sentiment. They struggled not only against Prussian contempt but also with the demands of conflicting nationalities within a decimated army.

Recriminations notwithstanding, Hindenburg and Ludendorff knew they had to relieve pressure on the Austro-Hungarian army or face collapse in Galicia. In October 1914 they took charge of the newly formed Ninth Army and attacked toward

Warsaw, only to be stopped by stiffening Russian resistance and worsening weather. But the thrust succeeded in relieving Russian pressure on the Austro-Hungarian lines. Hindenburg, after being named commander in chief of all German forces in the east (OberOst) on November 1, renewed the attack, this time in the direction of Lódz. Initial success was soon stymied by superior Russian numbers. The battle culminated in the hair-raising escape of General Reinhard von Scheffer-Boyadel's Twenty-fifth Reserve Corps from encirclement and near-certain annihilation. This high-wire act seemingly proved yet again that the Hindenburg–Ludendorff partnership was brilliant and unbeatable.

The audacious Lódz campaign in southern Poland—touted by the German press as rescuing Silesia from Russian invasion—earned Hindenburg his field marshal's baton on November 27. Throughout this nerve-wracking campaign Hindenburg remained "the personification of calm," steadying Ludendorff under the intense strain of constant fighting against superior numbers.[14]

Calm resolve at headquarters turned to stridency, however, as Hindenburg and Ludendorff's demands for reinforcements fell on Falkenhayn's deaf ears. If only they had possessed the forces that Falkenhayn profligately expended in futile assaults on the western front, Russia might already be facing calamitous defeat and begging for an armistice, or so Hindenburg and Ludendorff alleged. Much of the strategic plot of 1915 and 1916 on the German side revolved around the debate and infighting between "Westerners" led by Falkenhayn and "Easterners" led by Hindenburg and Ludendorff. Falkenhayn prevailed in part because he had the kaiser's confidence, but strategic disagreements between him and Hindenburg and Ludendorff soon became personal and increasingly bitter.

Hindenburg's arguments for further German offensives in the east were compelling. Here German forces could exploit their traditional strengths in mobility, flexibility, and improvisation. On the eastern front, where the force-to-space ratio was two thirds lower than in the west, breakthroughs could still be achieved. Roads were also fewer and more primitive and railroads less developed, complicating the ability of defenders to mobilize reserves. The east beckoned with promises of more Tannenbergs; the west promised more bloodlettings like Ypres.

As struggles to define Germany's military strategy raged behind the lines, Hindenburg strengthened his popular appeal by communicating forthrightly with the soldiers under his command. His general order of December 30, 1914, displayed all the hallmarks of a field marshal who possessed full confidence in himself and his army:

> Soldiers of the Eastern Army!
>
> It is my heart's desire to express to you my warmest thanks and my fullest recognition of what you have accomplished before the enemy during the year now closing. What privations you have borne, what forced marches you have made, what you have achieved in protracted and difficult fighting, will ever be accounted as among the greatest deeds in the military annals of all times. The days of Tannenberg, the Masurian Lakes . . . can never be forgotten.
>
> With thanks to God who gave us power to accomplish such things, and with a firm reliance upon his further help, let us begin the new year. In accordance with our oaths as soldiers we will continue to do our duty until our beloved Fatherland is assured of an honorable peace.
>
> And now let us go forward in 1915, just as in 1914.
>
> Long live His Majesty, our most gracious commander-in-chief! Hurrah![15]

As these inspiring words went forth, Hindenburg and Ludendorff schemed against Falkenhayn for control of Germany's strategy. As chief of the general staff, Falkenhayn possessed the formal authority to control deployments and determine Germany's overall military course. But Hindenburg, already compared to the mythic Siegfried on coins minted to commemorate Tannenberg, possessed enormous informal authority based on his victories and status as Germany's paradigmatic warrior-hero. As Falkenhayn tried to decapitate Hindenburg by reassigning Ludendorff to a newly created army in the east, Hindenburg strove to convince the kaiser to dismiss Falkenhayn. Supporters of Hindenburg recruited the empress and the kaiser's sons, among other luminaries, to his corner. Vexed to the point of tears, the kaiser considered court-martialing Hindenburg for insubordination.

Yet, Hindenburg was already the indispensable man—the unimpeachable savior of the fatherland. Across Germany he had become an icon—a man believed to possess the strength of character, commanding presence, and will to prevail. A heady concoction of militarism and romanticism made this a war of heroes, as *Junge Helden* (young heroes) performed *Heldentaten* (heroic deeds) in the *Heldenzone* (heroes' zone) at the front.[16] In private letters to his wife, Hindenburg admitted he was becoming a witting accomplice in the creation of his own heroic myth. Yet, he acquiesced because he knew Germany needed powerful myths if it was to triumph.

Unable to diminish Hindenburg, let alone dismiss him, the kaiser instead forged a compromise that pleased no one. He gave Ludendorff back to Hindenburg, together with three newly created army corps, but also kept Falkenhayn at his post. As a result, gossipy intriguers continued to haunt the corridors of OHL and OberOst, conspiring against one another and sowing the seeds of strategic disaster.

Early in 1915 Russia clarified German decision making by renewing attacks against East Prussia. In the second battle of the Masurian Lakes, German forces fighting in near white-out conditions, with snow up to their waists, prevailed and nearly annihilated the Russian Tenth Army. The bag included fifty-five thousand prisoners and a Russian corps commander. The campaign added so much to Hindenburg's luster that the kaiser felt constrained to remain in East Prussia so that he, not Hindenburg, might be considered its liberator.[17] The ploy fooled no one, highlighting instead Wilhelm's shortcomings even as a suitable figurehead for a total war.

Whereas the kaiser was flighty, insecure, and vain (Viennese wags wrote that he "insisted on being the stag at every hunt, the bride at every wedding and the corpse at every funeral"),[18] Hindenburg exuded confidence and spoke with dignified modesty. Incapable of providing firm and consistent direction, the kaiser was shunted aside. A substitute kaiser was needed to rally imperial Germany; Hindenburg inhabited the role as one to the manner born. His embodiment of Prussian and Lutheran virtues was enormously compelling; he seemed to spring from the very soil of Prussia. "One might compare Hindenburg to one of those big firmly-rooted oaks of the Prussian landscape under whose shade so many find protection and rest," his niece wrote. "He seemed to rise out of an old legend of our forefathers. He incorporated the soul of our nation, without being in the least self-conscious of it. And one felt awed at its tragic presence." Hyperbole and hagiography aside, this passage captured Germany's abiding affection for, even deification of, Hindenburg.[19]

Hindenburg became "the savior of the fatherland," a man who had selflessly answered his country's call to duty well after most men his age had retired. He came to symbolize mature masculinity to thousands of German men, themselves too old or infirm to serve at the front, who nevertheless could applaud one of their own giving his all. To women he was both loyal husband and loving father, demanding but fair, who would not waste the lives of their beloved men folk. To his soldiers he was courageous and steadfast in battle, honorable to enemies, compassionate to underlings. His love of the simple pleasures of life—good food, hunting, dogs—won him their affection. Larger than life, he nevertheless exhibited proper humility and modesty before God.

Character, rather than intellectual brilliance, was Hindenburg's core strength. His simplicity, his imposing physical presence, and especially his directness and devotion to duty endeared him to his soldiers and to the German people. He returned the favor, placing his trust in the strength and devotion of the German army. Had not the army prevailed against long odds in 1866 and 1870? Had not the army proven itself again in defeating the Russian hordes in 1914? To prevail in this latest war required *ora et labora*, work and prayer, enhanced by the skills of the hunter—patience, guile, and the resolution to squeeze the trigger at the right moment for a clean kill. Or so it seemed to Hindenburg.

Each major combatant in World War I needed a symbol to rally and reinforce national sentiment. In Britain it was Field Marshal Lord Earl Kitchener until his death in 1916. In France, the massive and phlegmatic Marshal Joseph Joffre inhabited the role until his decline in 1916. Multinational empires such as Austria-Hungary fought at a disadvantage, but the venerable Hapsburg emperor Franz Josef provided a rallying symbol until his death in 1916. Hindenburg, of course, fulfilled this essential role for Germany during and even after the war. His very name became synonymous with victory; those who spoke of a "Hindenburg peace" meant a victorious peace of conquest. His most mundane habits, even his *Abendtrunk,* or evening drink, became pregnant with new meaning: Just before his *Cercle* broke up each night, Hindenburg's adjutant squeezed a lemon into a glass and filled it with water. The great man then added sugar and stirred, noting dryly, "The secret is in the stirring." Sketching the scene with sacramental reverence was Hugo Vogel, the court painter.[20]

Hindenburg's image soon pervaded Germany. His determined visage was everywhere: on beer steins, pipes, coins, china, and ephemera such as postcards and recruiting posters.[21] Restaurants named their most ambitious culinary dishes after him. *Nagelsäulen* became totemic, even fetishistic, expressions of Hindenburg's virtues. Aides-de-camp posted to headquarters found themselves detailed to sorting baskets of mail and gifts sent daily to the Teutonic titan. It was once said that Napoleon's presence on the battlefield was equivalent to several divisions. One might say that Hindenburg's presence in Germany's collective psyche was at this stage of the war equivalent to several army corps.

"Brilliancy is not needed in war," Napoleon once noted, "only accuracy, character, and simplicity."[22] Hindenburg's stouthearted courage and firm resolution marked him as a man of character. An interview of Hindenburg conducted in February 1915 by the Progressive Republican and former U.S. senator Albert J. Beveridge highlighted Hindenburg's appeal. Beveridge was struck by Hindenburg's size: "broad-shouldered, thick-chested . . . the immense stature, the huge frame, the impression of tremendous, steady, unyielding force." "Here is a man," Beveridge concluded, "who makes up his mind what he wants or wants to do, and then has no further doubt on the subject. It is the kind of self-confidence that inspires confidence in others."

Consistent with his physical presence were Hindenburg's blunt and forthright views. Jealous of Germany's expanding power, England and its merchants were to blame for provoking a war, or so Hindenburg claimed. Instead of restraining Russian mobilization in July 1914, England had encouraged it, forcing Germany to strike to defend itself. Since the French army had already schemed to violate Belgian neutrality, Germany was more than justified in invading Belgium to come to grips with France.[23]

To Beveridge's assertion that militarism pervaded Germany and that many German soldiers were fighting "the kaiser's war" under duress, Hindenburg thundered, "The German army is the German people," and "The German Emperor and the German people are one." Showing unusual loquacity, he explained why Germany would prevail, despite the odds:

> Our knowledge that we are right; the faith of the nation that we shall win; their willingness to die in order to win; the perfect discipline of our troops; their understanding of orders; their greater intelligence, education and spirit; our organization and resources.[24]

Such rhetorical ruffles and flourishes were, of course, pitched for patriotic consumption. Yet, they also captured Hindenburg's absolute faith in the German army and people. And, they underscored his ability to use words calculated to swell listeners' hearts, thereby strengthening German resolve to attain victory, even if the cost should prove dear.

And the cost of war did prove dear, notably on the western front as each side dug in and extended the depth and complexity of its trench systems. Attacks by French and British forces in

1915 strained German resources but otherwise were ineffectual. Italian entry into the war against Austria-Hungary forced Conrad to divert men and matériel to the Isonzo. Fortunately for the Austrians, geography worked to frustrate Italian designs. Nevertheless, the need to rescue a faltering Hapsburg empire compelled a reluctant Falkenhayn to direct his attention eastwards in 1915.

After expelling Russian invaders from East Prussia early in 1915, Hindenburg and Ludendorff proposed a sweeping left-hook offensive, using no fewer than eight corps to surround and crush Russian forces in a salient centered on Warsaw. Combined with Austro-Hungarian attacks from Galicia, Hindenburg wanted to annihilate Russian forces in a huge *Kesselschlacht,* or cauldron battle. Falkenhayn vetoed this ambitious design as too risky for any likely gain, supporting instead a more limited operation, under General August von Mackensen, that relegated Hindenburg and Ludendorff to a secondary role.

In Mackensen's Gorlice-Tarnów Offensive in May, two million German and Austrian soldiers, supported by seven hundred thousand artillery rounds, shattered the Russian front line. The Central powers retook Galicia, advancing nearly two hundred miles along a seven-hundred-mile front from Riga to Pruth while inflicting three hundred thousand casualties on Russia. These were impressive figures, but Hindenburg and Ludendorff's grandiose design to effect another Cannae-like encirclement in Poland failed due to lack of manpower. Attacking out of East Prussia, Hindenburg nonetheless succeeded in taking Warsaw on August 4 and Pinsk and Vilna by September 18. Success earned him Oak Leaves for his *Pour le Mérite,* but when it came time for the kaiser to decorate him, Hindenburg was not favored with a postceremony drive in the kaiser's car. Fortune instead smiled on another officer so decorated, Hans von Beseler.[25]

This petty slight was symbolic of a dysfunctional system of high command. Continual conflicts over strategy revealed a lack of clarity and consensus within the general staff, OHL, and OberOst, let alone with Austria-Hungary. Competing viewpoints and an indecisive kaiser contributed to uncertainty. Each side in the debate played to its strong suit. Technocrats like Ludendorff strove to minimize uncertainty by achieving operational successes through tactical excellence, employing the best German troops in the east and seeking an end game based on decisive strategic victory to compel Russia to surrender. Falkenhayn and his fellow "Westerners," in contrast, focused on France and Britain. They tried to reduce forces in the east to the minimum needed to secure victories sufficiently one-sided to persuade the tsar to seek terms. What Hindenburg and Ludendorff saw as an end was for Falkenhayn only a means, with the result that no consistent strategy could be developed or executed.

Ironically, by limiting resources and reserves available to the east, Falkenhayn gave Hindenburg and Ludendorff a ready-made excuse for their inability to produce decisive results. They pointed to the two-hundred-mile retreat of Russian forces in Galicia; the occupation of Courland and Poland; and the entry of Bulgaria into the war on the side of the Central powers (Mackensen led a combined army that took Belgrade on October 9, 1915) to argue that the war was being won in the east. Yet, Falkenhayn remained unimpressed and noncommittal, not least because Russia refused to negotiate in spite of high losses. Faced with Falkenhayn's obduracy, Hindenburg and especially Ludendorff schemed to effect his dismissal. Aiding Ludendorff in his intrigue was Colonel Max Hoffmann, who bitterly referred to Falkenhayn as "that criminal."

Yet, Falkenhayn's pessimism about attaining a decision in the east was warranted. Million-man armies and vast spaces conspired to frustrate Frederician dreams of decisive battles. Diseases such as typhoid, cholera, and an epidemic of typhus cut into German combat strength. In the east, German units always seemed to face another day's march, with more Russian soldiers, clad in their earth-colored uniforms, at the end of it. The very behavior of Russian soldiers seemed incomprehensible. They might surrender in masses, white rags raised on the points of bayonets, and form themselves into columns to march off to captivity. Or they might fight fanatically to the end, with single machine gunners holding up whole battalions and soldiers without rifles resorting to rocks and fists. Their behavior seemed bewildering, even alien, when compared to French and British practices.

Hindenburg demonstrated his own set of unique behaviors. While Ludendorff slaved away at war making, Hindenburg kept to a regular schedule that included considerable time spent posing for portraits by Vogel, obsessing the while over trivial details of uniforms. Daily constitutional walks kept his health in good order. Brandy mellowed by age and champagne of German manufacture had a soothing effect. As his favorite foods became common knowledge among Germans, Hindenburg enjoyed a cornucopia of bottled eels, rusk (a sweetened biscuit), and pyramid cake. The gracious field marshal shared these delicacies with headquarters staff and visitors.

As the onset of winter froze operations in the east for 1915, Hindenburg and Ludendorff were put on ice as well. While Ludendorff fumed, Hindenburg went hunting. He was especially proud that winter of a bison he shot in the Russian forest of Bialovich, since one was depicted on his family's coat of arms. Such recreations may seem frivolous. They certainly drove hardworking subordinates to distraction and reinforced his reputation as a drone useful only for show. Earlier that September, Hoffmann cynically wrote that "we generally sign the orders 'von Hindenburg' without having shown them to him at all. The most brilliant commander of all times no longer has the slightest interest in military matters; Ludendorff does everything himself."[26] But doing "everything" led to micromanagement; Ludendorff exhausted himself as he directed operations in the east while intriguing against Falkenhayn in the west.

As Ludendorff wrestled with enemies real and imagined, it might seem as if Hindenburg had become merely a château general. Yet, Hindenburg recognized the importance of wholesome exercise in the field and its reinforcement of his image as a warrior. He recognized as well the risks of micromanagement—increasingly characteristic of all combatants in this bureaucratized war. Where no major decisions were to be made, it was folly for a commander in chief to dissipate energy in details. "Those who have the best nerves," Hindenburg declared, "will win the war."[27] But there was more to this war than keeping one's nerve.

Despite fractious contests of will and differing strategic aims, the Central powers had worked fairly well together in 1915. Prospects for the new year looked bright. Conrad suggested a general offensive to eliminate Italy from the war, after which Austria-Hungary would join with Germany to finish Russia. Hindenburg and Ludendorff ignored Italy and instead argued for a massive attack to fell a teetering Russian Empire. Falkenhayn rejected both. Fed up with criticism that he had failed to grasp total military victory in the east, which even yet lay within reach, Falkenhayn turned westwards. Arguing that France was nearing the end of its endurance militarily and economically, Falkenhayn decided to drive the French from the war, not by seeking a decisive breakthrough in the style of 1914, but by choosing an objective for whose retention the French must commit their remaining resources. Two such sites existed: the fortresses of Belfort and Verdun. Verdun, laden with historic and emotional significance for France, seemed more promising.[28] Here Falkenhayn could control the campaign without having to share credit with the Hindenburg-Ludendorff team and without having to coordinate action with the gloomy Conrad and his lackluster army. By placing Crown Prince Wilhelm in command of the offensive, Falkenhayn also sought to restore luster to the tarnished Hohenzollern crown and thereby to diminish the ranks of those who idolized Hindenburg.

Hindenburg and Ludendorff watched resentfully from the sidelines as Falkenhayn launched the attack at Verdun on February 21, 1916. It remains a subject of scholarly controversy whether Falkenhayn intended to defeat France by bleeding its army white in the trenches or by convincing the French government and people that the war was unwinnable. Either intention involved commitment to an *Ermattungsstrategie* (strategy of exhaustion), a concept hitherto anathema to German generals, who sought Armageddon in quick time.

Falkenhayn made two costly errors. First, he chose not to co-ordinate strategy with Austria-Hungary, thereby sacrificing whatever trust still lingered between his and Conrad's respective staffs. Second, Falkenhayn chose not to share his strategy with his own army commanders. Once inflamed, Germany's national pride subverted his goal of minimizing German casualties while inflicting unsustainable casualties on Entente forces. The deci-sion to conceal his intent at Verdun—Falkenhayn later stated he never intended to capture the city at all—meant that Verdun be-came "sacred soil" for the Germans as well as the French. Geo-graphic features like Fort Douaumont and Dead Man's Hill acquired totemic status, with physical and moral consequences amplified by the massive British offensive at the Somme begin-ning in July. Aiming for a casualty ratio of 2.5:1 in his favor, Falkenhayn accepted instead a grim 1.2:1. The Germans gave better than they got, but it was they who could least afford the exchange.

Verdun, in Winston Churchill's words, may have been a vic-tory "so dear as to be almost indistinguishable from defeat," but it was nevertheless a French victory. Like Tannenberg it spawned its own sustaining mythology, symbolized by the *Voie Sacrée,* or Sacred Way (the road the French used to funnel men and matériel to Verdun) and General Henri-Philippe Pétain's im-mortal words, "*Ils ne passeront pas!*" (They shall not pass). Be-lated efforts by Hindenburg to praise Verdun as a "beacon light of German valor" paled in comparison to Pétain's *cri de coeur.* Verdun proved to be an abattoir not just for the French army but for the German as well. Even worse, Falkenhayn's devious deci-sion to hide Verdun's intent eroded the moral underpinnings of the German army.

Exacerbating Falkenhayn's moral and military failure at Ver-dun was Russian general Alexei Brusilov's breakout offensive in Galicia in June. By July Russian forces had retaken Galicia and the Bukovina, capturing nearly half a million demoralized Aus-

d resolve they could muster. Hindenburg's strai
stiff-like countenance, and his heroic image inspi
tion, and further exertions. It remained to be s
and Ludendorff could guide Germany to victory
ll of 1916, Hindenburg and Ludendorff's first prio
alize the empire's war efforts. Despite two years o
at and horrendous casualties, the Great War see
to a conclusion for either side. After touring
Verdun in September, a subdued Hindenburg w
n soldiers "hardly ever saw anything but trenches
. . . for weeks and even months. . . . I could now
ow everyone, officers and men alike, longed to
such an atmosphere." Doubtless recalling his own
66 and 1870, Hindenburg wrote sadly of how sol
ounce that mighty spiritual exaltation which acc
ctorious advance. . . . How many of our brave
known this, the purest of a soldier's joys."³
, Hindenburg noted, had become a colossal *Ma*
r material struggle, waged by modern industrial
he western front in particular witnessed orga
on a scale theretofore thought impossible. Stagg
r wastage of modern war, all combatants sought
rees of success to mobilize their economies. Th
denburg Program was Germany's concerted att
fully, if somewhat belatedly, for total war.
ng the efficiency of economic mobilization was
rthwhile goal. Hindenburg's, and especially Lu
mistake was to presume that an economy coul
d like an army. The end result was a conflict of
hat was best for the army in the short term wa
best for the long-term health of the economy.
s economic means were mobilized to the fulles
quired and incurred by modern warfare's destru
m drove Germany, as well as the Entente powe
tegic goals to justify national sacrifice. Extreme
bilization encouraged grandiose political and te

trian soldiers. Austria's collapse encouraged Rumania's entry into the war on the side of the Entente in August. Upon learning of Rumania's declaration of war, a hysterical kaiser cried that Germany had lost the war. He spoke two years too soon.

For Germany the tragedy was that, had Falkenhayn foregone Verdun to aid Austria-Hungary in its campaign against Italy, chances were excellent that Italy would have been forced from the war. Conrad could then have redeployed forces from Italy to the eastern front in time to blunt Brusilov's offensive. Instead, Falkenhayn and Conrad went separate ways, both launching offensives against different foes, and both weakening their forces in the east. Their uncoordinated actions set the stage for Russia's greatest victory of the war. Brusilov's offensive, together with the British offensive at the Somme, prevented Falkenhayn from keeping sufficient pressure on the French army to bleed it white. Instead, the German army came close to bleeding itself white on the ravaged slopes overlooking Verdun. As the army lost its vitality, so too did Falkenhayn.

Having refused to sanction Hindenburg and Ludendorff's calls for Falkenhayn's dismissal, the kaiser took notice when Bethmann Hollweg joined the anti-Falkenhayn chorus. Writing to General Moritz Baron von Lyncker on June 23, 1916, the chancellor noted, "The name Hindenburg frightens our enemies, galvanizes our army and people, which have boundless confidence in him. . . . If we were to lose a battle, which God forbid, our people would [nevertheless] accept it, and likewise any peace to which he put his name."²⁹ Falkenhayn's name possessed none of these magical qualities, a fact even the kaiser was forced to admit.

Early in July, Falkenhayn confronted Hindenburg about his ambition for the post of chief of the general staff, reportedly saying, "Well, if Herr Field Marshal has the desire and the courage to take the post." Hindenburg's reply, "The desire, no, but the courage—yes," was perfectly judged.³⁰ An emotional kaiser nevertheless shed tears when faced with the crushing decision to replace Falkenhayn. Recognizing that the game was up,

Falkenhayn saluted the kaiser, then bowed to Hindenburg and offered his hand, saying "God help you and our Fatherland." He ignored Ludendorff, who nevertheless earned his own promotion and the newly created title of first quartermaster general. From September 1916 to October 1918, Ludendorff was the man most directly responsible for the German army's daily conduct of the war. Ludendorff further insisted that he share with Hindenburg responsibility for all decisions rendered. It was not lost on anyone that the date was August 29, 1916, the second anniversary of Tannenberg.

Writing soon after the war, the young Charles de Gaulle put it aptly, "The old Prussians of the right loved the warrior puritanism of Hindenburg and Ludendorff—their religion of effort; their unlimited contempt for all that was not Prussian, Lutheran, and soldierly; their inflexible confidence in the patriotic use of force and fraud."[31] But as Hew Strachan has noted, the new team bought Germany only a set of attitudes and images. The Second Reich still had no machinery for supreme command. "Without it, [Germany] had no capacity for the sustained integration of war and foreign policy."[32] And that in turn was a recipe for defeat no less certain for requiring time.

# Supreme Comm

W HEN SHE fi
1916, Marion Dönhoff was u
stiff gait and oddly short steps
looked more like the Nutcracke
imagination," confessed the y
however, wholeheartedly embr
were thrilled to learn of his ap
staff. Earlier that August, Lie
how Hindenburg's previous
mander in the east had come "
never to have had a reverse.
Hanseatickers, Mechlinburger
wild with joy at the news." Ka
front in October, echoed these
through Cambrai," Gorzel w
greeted him with exultant chee
our limbs like fire and filled us
ing endured hard fighting in t
tings at Verdun and the Somm

courage a
talk, his m
trust, affe
whether h
In the f
was to revi
tense com
no closer
Somme ar
that Germ
shell holes
derstand
away from
ploits in 1
had "to re
panies a
have neve
The w
alschlacht,
gernauts.
destructio
by the she
varying d
called Hi
to mobili
Improv
tainly a
dorff's, k
command
ciencies.
necessaril
thermore,
sacrifices
industrial
inflate str
nomic m

rial demands, ruling out opportunities for a compromise peace, which Hindenburg and Ludendorff rejected anyway. Under their leadership, imperial Germany became a machine for waging war and little else. And Hindenburg and Ludendorff emerged as Germany's most committed merchants of death.

Nothing in Hindenburg's background prepared him for the task of overseeing an economic mobilization. Thus, he left details to the technocrat Ludendorff. Aided by Lieutenant Colonel Max Bauer, Ludendorff embarked on a crash program to centralize and streamline the economy. Fifteen separate district commands in Germany needed centralizing if economic mobilization was to be rationalized; rivalries among federal, state, and local agencies needed to be curtailed. As enacted, the Hindenburg Program sought to maximize war-related production by transforming Germany into a garrison state with a command economy. Coordinating the massive effort was the *Kriegsamt,* or War Office, headed by General Wilhelm Groener.

Yet, Ludendorff's insistence on setting unachievable production goals led to serious dislocations in the national economy. Shell production was to be doubled, artillery and machine gun production trebled, all in a matter of months. The German economy, relying largely on its own internal resources, could not bear the strain of striving for production goals unconstrained by economic, material, and manpower realities. The release of hundreds of thousands of skilled workers from military duty back to the factories, which led to short-term increases in the production of armaments, did not solve critical and systemic shortages of labor. Large-scale deportation and impressment of Belgian workers was a stopgap that only further alienated world opinion, notably in the United States. In the aggregate, the high level of autonomy enjoyed by the military contributed to wasteful duplications of effort and patterns of bureaucratization that eventually defied even the Germans' gift for paperwork.

As industrialists fought for limited resources in futile attempts to meet Ludendorff's unrealistic production goals, shortages of food in Germany led to altered diets, increasing the physical and mental fatigue of workers and their families. Food riots broke out in Berlin as early as October 1915. By 1916 inflation was making it difficult for workers to afford the bare necessities. Germans before the war on the whole lived well, with high average consumptions of meat, white bread, and beer. A disastrous harvest in the fall of 1916 led to the *Kohlrübenwinter* (turnip winter) of 1916–1917 and a diet even leaner in meats and fats. By the winter of 1917–1918, meat and butter allocations dropped to one fifth of prewar consumption levels. Turnip derivatives and similar ersatz products were unpalatable substitutes.[4] The average German may not have been starving, but he believed he was.[5] Exacerbating shortages in basic staples was a distribution network that worked capriciously when it did work, leading to inequities in burden sharing, recriminations at local levels, and the proliferation of black markets and general lawlessness.

Heightening the strains of grandiose production goals and resource inequities for ordinary citizens was the marked tendency of imperial authorities to treat citizens as subjects who had to put up and shut up. Ludendorff and his economic deputies focused more on manufacturing guns than on negotiating consent. Such heavy-handedness ordinary Germans could tolerate as long as news from the front remained favorable. Because they believed victory was ultimately still theirs, especially with the heroes of Tannenberg now in charge, ordinary Germans grumbled but persevered. But the duumvirate's decision to rely on military victories to manufacture consent ran the obvious risk of moral breakdown if and when news from the front turned sour.

A further element of the Hindenburg Program was the *Hilfsdienstgesetz* (Patriotic Auxiliary Service Law). Passed by the Reichstag in December 1916, the law extended national service to men as young as seventeen and as old as sixty. It also restricted workers' mobility, to which labor consented only by forcing concessions of their own, including the right to organize in war industries and to determine jointly with management the fate of individual workers who contested orders to move. Further estranging workers were hardnosed policy statements that went out under Hindenburg's signature. One such statement declared that women who failed to contribute to the war effort, even soldiers' widows, should expect to go hungry.[6] Barking commands to grieving widows was not the way to win hearts and minds. Few German civilians relished being treated as interchangeable cogs in an indifferent military machine.

For the moment, sociopolitical tensions and economic shortages remained within tolerable limits on the home front, especially as the German army recovered from military reverses it endured earlier in 1916. Ironically, it was the demoted Falkenhayn, together with Mackensen, who oversaw the defeat of Rumanian forces and the capture of Bucharest in December 1916. (The theatrical Mackensen rode triumphantly into the city on a white horse.) Rumania's entry into the war, initially inducing nervous prostration in the kaiser, ultimately helped rather than hurt the resource-starved Central powers. Once defeated and occupied, the full range of Rumania's products—notably oil and wheat—became available. Meanwhile, Russian forces, in covering a new flank, were stretched even thinner.

As they restored the military situation in the east, Hindenburg and Ludendorff recognized Germany had to stand on the defensive in the west. Discontinuing the offensive at Verdun, they consolidated forces in preparation for the expected Anglo-French offensive in the spring of 1917. Their wisest decision was to shorten German lines on the western front by withdrawing forces quietly and gradually to a prebuilt and elastic system of defense in depth. Known as the Siegfried Line to the Germans and the Hindenburg Line to the Entente powers, the new system consisted of a thinly held outpost zone designed to minimize friendly soldiers' exposure to enemy artillery barrages. A main battle zone that incorporated ferroconcrete pillboxes, elaborate trench systems, and dense concentrations of wire protected by tank traps presented the main obstacle to attackers. Beginning in February 1917, German forces withdrew to new positions, shortening their lines by twenty-five miles and freeing up a mobile reserve of thirteen divisions. Caught off guard by this withdrawal, Entente forces advanced warily across shell-blasted, booby-trapped terrain.[7]

The German army's withdrawal to the Hindenburg Line was masterful. Yet, two decisions with enormous political implications were bungled. The first of these was Ludendorff's decision to revive the kingdom of Poland. Seduced by visions of Polish armies wreaking havoc in Russia, Ludendorff instead had to settle for a couple of ineffective divisions. Polish leaders were no fools; neither were their soldiers, who did not relish serving as cannon fodder for German ambitions. Announcement of the new kingdom on November 5, 1916, meanwhile, eliminated chances for a compromise peace with Russia in 1917. Instead, Russia collapsed into Bolshevism, a contagion that soon spread to the German army in 1918.

As this political débâcle unfolded, the relentless Entente naval blockade continued to bite into the German home front. At Jutland the German navy's most concerted effort to break the blockade ended in failure. Submarine warfare against Britain was hamstrung by rules of war that required boarding and searching merchant vessels prior to sinking them. Obedience to these regulations appeased complaints from the United States stemming from the sinking of the *Lusitania* in 1915 and the *Sussex* in 1916, but they also compromised U-boats' effectiveness while increasing risks for their crews. As 1916 closed, the German navy argued strenuously for unrestricted and unremitting U-boat attacks against Entente and neutral shipping to force Britain to sue for peace.

With the High Seas Fleet bottled up in port, German naval advocates led by the retired Admiral Alfred von Tirpitz and Admiral Henning von Holtzendorff, the chief of the naval staff, argued that in six months U-boats could sink enough ships to weaken fatally Britain's will to continue the fight. Given the small number of ocean-going U-boats Germany had on hand (often fewer than thirty patrolling the waters around the British Isles), it was a gamble at long odds. Seeing no other way out of a

*Materialschlacht* on multiple fronts, Hindenburg and Ludendorff approved in January 1917 an end game that relied on an improvised maritime strategy—a *guerre à outrance* against Entente and neutral shipping off of Britain's coastline. Such were the strategic depths to which the vaunted genius of the German general staff had sunk.[8]

Coincidentally, in February 1917 Walter Nernst, the Nobel Prize winning physicist, won an audience with the kaiser. If unrestricted submarine warfare drove the United States to declare war on Germany, Nernst warned, American money, industry, and men would sustain the Entente as Germany's resources continued to shrink. With considerable probity, perhaps because of his detachment from daily war fighting, Nernst advised the kaiser to seek a negotiated settlement while Germany was still strong. Ludendorff, with Hindenburg nodding alongside, dismissed Nernst's advice as "the incompetent nonsense of a civilian."[9] With the kaiser's blessing, they persevered in seeking total victory through unrestricted submarine warfare.[10]

In sinking neutral shipping indiscriminately, Hindenburg and Ludendorff knew they would compel Woodrow Wilson, re-elected president of the United States in 1916 on the slogan "He Kept Us Out of War," to ask Congress for a declaration of war against Germany, which he did in April 1917. They gambled that Germany's army and U-boats would mortally wound the Entente powers before U.S. soldiers reached France in significant numbers. They failed to appreciate fully, however, that America's very entry took the Entente off of life support.

This decision cost Germany the war. Many events on land went Germany's way in 1917: the French general Robert Nivelle's unimaginative and stubborn assaults on the Hindenburg Line in April that ended in widespread mutiny within the French army; the British Expeditionary Force's (BEF) fall into the "slough of despond" at Third Ypres (Passchendaele) from July to November; the collapse of Italian forces at Caporetto in October; and, most signally, Russia's political revolution and subsequent departure from the war.[11] Anglo-French forces reeled under these blows but refused to break precisely because they knew "the Yanks were coming." So focused were Hindenburg and Ludendorff on steeling the will of the German army that they failed to see how their drive for victory by any means was simultaneously preserving the will of Germany's enemies.

Forever seeking a knockout battle—a greater Cannae—German strategists should have instead recalled the Peloponnesian War. Here Sparta—a tough, militaristic empire based on land power—cobbled together an effective coalition to humble the democratic, but arrogant, Athenian Empire. Like the Spartans, Hindenburg and his fellow *Junkers* valued martial skill and willpower. But, whereas Athenian arrogance had aided Sparta in its recruitment of allies, in this case it was Germany who was arrogant. As Germany rode roughshod over Austria-Hungary's concerns, the latter looked for an exit. Only Germany's wholesale takeover of Austro-Hungarian forces in 1917 salvaged the situation, but at the price of a predictable attenuation of German combat power. Entente forces, in contrast, developed mechanisms, however imperfect, for cooperation that culminated in the appointment of a supreme commander, the French general Ferdinand Foch, in 1918.

Telling here was Hindenburg's backhanded compliment of the British Empire. Comparing Britain to another classical paradigm, that of the Roman Empire, Hindenburg wrote after the war of Britain's "ruthless selfishness which scorned no method of dealing with friend or foe where her own interests were concerned, her virtuous indignation, skillfully staged, whenever her enemies paid her back in her own coin." Britain's statesmen, Hindenburg ruefully admitted, "succeeded in developing all these aspects of the diplomatic art to the highest pitch of refinement and duplicity."[12] Echoes of "Perfidious Albion," perhaps, but Britain's leaders made politics and warfare serve each other far more effectively than did Germany's warlords.

Demonstrating Britain's superior diplomatic finesse, especially in the United States, was its carefully tuned propaganda, to which Germany's ham-fisted Zimmermann telegram made a signal contribution.[13] Efforts to seek Mexico's cooperation in early 1917 were both ill timed and poorly implemented. Britain took full advantage, publicizing the text of the German foreign office's offer of an alliance and financial support in return for a Mexican offensive to recover Texas, New Mexico, and Arizona. An American public, which had been "too proud to fight," now sought to avenge both the telegram and indiscriminate U-boat attacks.

In this difficult hour, the Second Reich needed a second Bismarck to emerge, a master diplomat possessing the guile and force of will to corral an unruly and demanding OHL. Somehow this paragon would also have had to square the circle by negotiating an end to the war on terms acceptable to all combatants. It is perhaps enough to state the task to show the impossibility of Bethmann Hollweg's meeting it. It is certain that Hindenburg and Ludendorff—the de facto rulers of Germany—only knew how to wage war, not how to end it.

Before the war, the kaiser had declared, "The soldiers and the army, not parliamentary majorities and decisions, have welded the German Empire together. I put my trust in the army." Now Hindenburg and Ludendorff, neither of whom the kaiser liked nor trusted, commanded that army. Indeed, the kaiser envied Hindenburg's iconic status and worried he was becoming "the people's tribune." And the Hindenburg–Ludendorff tribunal was not above blackmailing their emperor to get their way. As they sought to win a "Hindenburg peace," they confronted a political landscape that was fractured within, as well as between, political parties. Elements in the Reichstag clamored for an armistice that would restore the *status quo ante bellum*. Conspiring to silence these "defeatist" elements, Hindenburg and Ludendorff inverted Clausewitz, making politics the continuation of war by other means.

To this end Hindenburg lent his imprimatur to the *Vaterlands-Partei* (Fatherland Party), a rightist and reactionary organization headed by Tirpitz and Wolfgang Kapp (later ringleader of the abortive Kapp Putsch in 1920). All appetite and grievances, within a year of its formal creation on Sedan Day in September 1917 the Fatherland Party counted a million members within its ranks. Its comprehensive annexationist platform particularly attracted Hindenburg, who since his initial victories in 1914 had entertained thoughts of a postwar *Ostimperium* (eastern empire), an endless source of human and material resources to be exploited for the Reich.[14]

Hindenburg and Ludendorff were imperialists, to be sure. But they were soldiers first. They favored military solutions to political problems. A hammer was their one tool, so all problems became nails to be driven into submission. Bethmann Hollweg now became one of these nails, even though he had supported Hindenburg's appointment as chief of the general staff. As the chancellor tried to play both ends against the middle, sympathizing with socialists and efforts at franchise reform while also paying lip service to decisive victory and the will to prevail, Hindenburg and Ludendorff schemed to isolate him and remove him from power.

During his one, shining moment, the kaiser famously declared in August 1914 that he knew no political parties, only Germans. Under the *Burgfrieden* (literally, peace within the castle walls), open political dissent in Germany had been squelched by mutual consent of the leading political parties. Unprecedented stresses from constant fighting on multiple fronts, however, revealed the fault lines in Germany's political landscape. As Pan-Germans and other conservative elements worked for an annexationist and acquisitive victory, Social Democrats, Catholic Centrists, and Progressives sought to end the war without annexations or indemnities. Further dividing these parties was the question of suffrage; more liberal elements wanted to eliminate the three-tier voting system in Prussia that favored traditional elites. Bethmann Hollweg's mistake was to adopt a compromise position that pleased no one, least of all rabid annexationists like Ludendorff.

Hindenburg was less hungry for the spoils of war, even poking fun at those Germans who dreamed of the *Mona Lisa* gracing the Berlin Museum and of Ceylon as a colonial jewel in the imperial crown. Yet, he could not countenance the growing assertiveness of a Reichstag in pursuit of peace without victory. As he was a soldier, such political concerns should have fallen outside his purview. A firm precedent for military dominance of traditionally civilian sectors, however, had already been established at the beginning of mobilization.[15]

Hindenburg worked both to preserve the army's paramount place in German society and the ideal of the state as a monarchy invested with the authority of a people who freely placed their trust in the kaiser. Yet, as the kaiser proved irresolute, a victim of incapacitating depressions and hysterical collapses, Hindenburg found himself becoming an *ersatz kaiser,* thereby actualizing Wilhelm's worst fear. Deciding that no equivocation could be tolerated, Hindenburg concluded Bethmann Hollweg had to go.

As the Reichstag prepared to flex atrophied muscles, Hindenburg acted, petitioning the kaiser on June 27, 1917, that his greatest fear was "the decline in the national spirit. It must be revived, or we shall lose the war."[16] Ludendorff followed with specifics, blaming Bethmann Hollweg for abetting "German Radical Social Democracy" and its "longing for peace." By refusing to suppress radical socialists, the chancellor allowed an "ax [to be] laid to the tree of the Imperial Office and the glory of the Empire," Ludendorff concluded.

Collectively, the warlords tendered their resignation to the kaiser on July 12, 1917, knowing he could not afford to accept it. Their act, however, compelled Bethmann Hollweg to resign the next day. For his replacement, Hindenburg and Ludendorff settled on Georg Michaelis, formerly under secretary of state and director of the Wartime Food Office. An efficient if colorless bureaucrat, Michaelis was easily dominated by OHL. (Bauer openly referred to Michaelis as "chancellor of the OHL.") In deferring to OHL's recommendation, the kaiser essentially granted Hindenburg and Ludendorff the power to fire and hire chancellors at will.

Supporting Bethmann Hollweg's dismissal were the Social

Democratic Party (SDP), the Catholic Center Party, and the Progressive People's Party, who viewed him as a stumbling block to peace. With him gone, they pressed ahead with a peace resolution, but it was already dead on arrival. Hindenburg and Ludendorff, who had successfully conspired to reduce the chancellor's position to that of scapegoat to distract people from their grievances, were not about to acquiesce in a compromise peace.[17]

While neutering the chancellor's position and neutralizing the Reichstag, Hindenburg and Ludendorff also worked to revitalize military spirit and morale via a program of *Vaterländischer Unterricht* (patriotic instruction). In war, the first casualty has always been truth. But this new program took dissembling over the line to a systematic campaign of lies. German casualty figures were underreported, in particular by excluding those treated at frontline dressing stations and returned to duty. In official communiqués and newspaper accounts, defeats became setbacks; setbacks became redeployments. On the home front OHL reported no lack of food even as people scraped to find enough to feed their children.

Widespread anger and cynicism, of a depth foreign to the war's early years, was the most important result of this campaign of lies. One soldier in 1917 wrote, "Messrs. Pan-Germans sit on the high horse. But they may be glad that we don't pull them off their big estates. . . . Starvation makes me whistle: *Hunger über alles in der Welt.*" Other soldiers groused that the acronym "kv," meaning fit for frontline service, actually meant *keine Verbindung,* or no (political) pull. The acronym "gv," fit for garrison duty, became *gute Verbindung,* or good pull. Safest of all was "av," fit for labor service, which became *ausgezeichnete Verbindung,* or excellent pull.[18] The enthusiastic volunteers of 1914 had become the resentful *Frontschweine* (front pigs) of 1917, accepting ever-greater burdens in a war whose end seemed increasingly uncertain.

There is little doubt that Hindenburg and Ludendorff achieved military excellence on land in 1917. But at what cost to

Germany's soldiers? Nearly a million men were already dead. Casualties were likely to be returned to hospitals, asylums, and convalescent homes in Germany, if for no better reason than to make room at field hospitals for the next intake of broken minds and bodies. Soldiers on furlough confronted the visible consequences of a rationing system that allowed those with money to purchase luxury items virtually at will. They saw disabled comrades regarded as public embarrassments, particularly *les grandes mutilés* (the severely maimed) produced by the combination of modern high explosives and modern medical techniques.[19] A discreet cast or sling was one thing for the good burghers of Mainz or Berlin. A limbless torso was quite another.

With Russia's collapse, prospects for victory brightened, however, as Germans came together in October to celebrate Hindenburg's seventieth birthday. Getting wind of the festivities planned in his honor, Hindenburg implored his fellow Germans to remember instead wounded soldiers and their dependents. But a chance to rally support for the war was not to be missed. That second day of October, children got a day off from school, villages and towns across the Reich held festivals, and the kaiser extended his personal thanks to Germany's greatest wartime hero. Hindenburg's reaction to the kaiser's gift of his own bust in marble went unrecorded; compared to his warlords, the kaiser had become little more than a lifeless monument.[20]

To Hindenburg it seemed an appropriate occasion to issue a ringing manifesto. He promptly did so, repeating the myth that Germany was fighting a defensive war, which nevertheless would lead to *Lebensraum* (living space) for "free growth":

> With God's help our German strength has withstood the tremendous attack of our enemies, because we were one, because each gave his all gladly. So it must stay to the end. 'Now thank we all our God' on the bloody battlefield! Take no thought for what is to be after the war! This only brings despondency into our ranks and strengthens the hopes of the enemy. Trust that Germany will achieve what she needs to stand there safe for all time, trust that the German oak will be given air and light for its free growth! Muscles tensed, nerves

steeled, eyes front! We see before us the aim: Germany honored, free and great! God will be with us to the end![21]

Ostensibly fighting a defensive war for *Gott, Kaiser und Vaterland*, Hindenburg actually sacrificed his men to create a new Germania. In the west it included annexation of the Low Countries and the channel coast as well as the subjugation of France. With the collapse of tsarist Russia, Hindenburg further sought sweeping annexations in the east (including the Baltic provinces, Poland, and all of Ukraine) that amounted to an evisceration of the fallen Russian Empire.

In marginalizing and muzzling the Reichstag and monopolizing power, Hindenburg and Ludendorff contemptuously dismissed both the will of the people and the value of diplomacy. A compromise peace might still have been possible in 1917, when Germany could have negotiated from a position of strength. Instead, Hindenburg and Ludendorff drove their country into the ground. The barren soil they left behind was far more hospitable to the hardy weeds of fascism than to the fragile flowers of parliamentary democracy.

As German strategy evolved from deterrence in the 1880s to doomsday machine by 1914, stated war aims changed from defensive struggle in 1914 to voracious *Weltpolitik* by 1917. A few major defeats may have forced Hindenburg and Ludendorff to confront their limitations. Instead, a string of impressive, if indecisive, victories bred hubris, leading Hindenburg to declare, "The relations between me and my soldiers are as they should be—love for love, trust for trust—relations which are bound to ensure victory."[22] As the self-appointed tribunes of Germany discovered in 1918, victory is never assured, and the gods of war rarely fail to punish hubris.

# Collapse and Catastrophe, 1918

Reviewing the events of 1916 and 1917, Hindenburg and Ludendorff deserve credit for restoring German morale by returning to the defensive on the western front while driving Russia from the war both by intensifying Russia's own internal discord and by employing new assault tactics, depending on shock and dislocation rather than attrition, at Riga, Caporetto, and Cambrai.[1] In contrast to a French army recovering from widespread mutiny and an exhausted and bedraggled BEF, a reinvigorated German army looked forward to victory. Yet, the failure of unrestricted submarine warfare to knock Britain out of the war revealed Hindenburg and Ludendorff's Achilles' heel: They lacked a grand strategy to win the war. Their focus remained operational in nature. Indeed, Ludendorff's basic understanding of war remained at the level of a regimental colonel.[2]

As 1918 opened Germany still had the option of seeking a favorable conclusion to the war through negotiation. By offering to end the submarine campaign, withdraw from all or most of its conquests in the west, and reaffirm the kaiser's earlier guarantee of Belgium's integrity, Germany could have shifted the burden to the Entente: Agree to bargain or take the blame for a repeat of the slaughters of 1917. This approach would also have bought time for Germany to consolidate its eastern conquests while shoring up a home front that was showing serious signs of strain.

Yet, the conference to define Germany's strategy for 1918 had already been held at Mons on November 11, 1917. Remarkably, no civilians were present, not even the chancellor. Nor was the kaiser or even Hindenburg present. Ludendorff chaired the meeting of Germany's senior army commanders. Having endured yet another bloodletting at Third Ypres and recognizing that American soldiers would arrive in large numbers by the summer of 1918, Ludendorff insisted that Germany's only path to decisive victory was an all-out offensive in the spring. The key issue in Ludendorff's mind was to identify the correct sector of the western front to pulverize. In retrospect, what did not work in 1914 (the Schlieffen Plan), with the advantage of surprise, could hardly be expected to work in 1918.

General Wilhelm Groener had his finger on the pulse of Germany when he noted in 1917 that Hindenburg and Ludendorff were not statesmen, yet by default they were entrusted with making the peace. But they were infected by victory disease. At a Crown Council held in February 1918, the kaiser discussed Russia's partition into four lesser empires. Hindenburg declared he needed the Baltic States for the maneuvering of his left wing in the next war. Ludendorff suggested annexations ranging as far as the Caspian Sea. It was perhaps appropriate that the meeting took place at a sanitarium—the dialogue at Bad Homburg matched for absurd abstractions anything held on Thomas Mann's *Magic Mountain*. The discourse reflected, however, a developed consciousness of the East as a source of power—perhaps even the mythic successor to the United States as a "land of limitless possibilities."[3] Not content with mere incremental aggrandizement, Hindenburg and Ludendorff sought to consolidate eastern and central Europe into an empire that could serve as a stable base for the expected next round of conflict.

As cooler heads such as the septuagenarian Georg Count von

Hertling, formerly minister president of Bavaria and now chancellor with the demise of Georg Michaelis, argued for a less onerous peace and an equitable sharing of eastern spoils with Austria-Hungary, Hindenburg and Ludendorff once again threw down the gauntlet. In a letter dated January 7, 1918, Hindenburg made an emotive appeal to the kaiser. "Your Majesty," Hindenburg wrote, "will not order honest men who have served Your Majesty and the Fatherland faithfully to attach the weight of their names and authority to proceedings which their innermost conviction tells them to be harmful to the Crown and the Empire."[4] Disingenuously and self-servingly, Hindenburg claimed that soldiers preparing for the upcoming "victory offensive" in the west needed to see sweeping territorial gains in the east, else their motivation to fight and faith in the kaiser would be compromised, perhaps fatally.

Wilhelm II, reduced to a *Schattenkaiser* (shadow emperor), was unprepared to risk any slackening of Germany's fighting spirit. Once again the duumvirate prevailed. Two days later, Hindenburg crowed to Hertling that he was glad "it has now been decided to be firm at Brest-Litovsk and to speak to the Russians in the language of the conqueror."[5] The resulting Treaty of Brest-Litovsk ignored Wilson's Fourteen Points of January and confirmed in Western eyes the insatiable appetite of German militarism.

Under the terms of the treaty, signed by communist Russia under duress on March 3, 1918, Germany acquired the Baltic provinces, Finland, White Russia, Ukraine, and ancillary territories—nearly four hundred thousand square miles populated by forty-five million people. Besides losing one third of its population, Russia lost half its industrial base and nearly 90 percent of its coal mines. Leon Trotsky, leader of the nascent Red Army, vowed immediate vengeance, declaring that Brest-Litovsk was merely an armistice until the next round of fighting. Even harsher than Brest-Litovsk was the Treaty of Bucharest against Rumania. Signed on May 7, 1918, the treaty made Rumania a vassal of the Central powers. Terms included military occupation, German control both of Rumania's oil reserves for ninety-nine years and of navigation on the Danube, as well as the ceding of substantial swathes of Rumanian territory to Austria-Hungary.

The spoils from both treaties proved temporary, however. To enforce the terms, Germany had to keep three dozen divisions in the east. Even as trench holders these units would have been better employed in the great offensive pending in the west. After extended exposure to Bolshevik propaganda, many of these units became politically unreliable and had to be kept in the east in the political equivalent of a quarantine.

In coercing sweeping concessions from Russia and Rumania, Hindenburg and Ludendorff's reach exceeded their grasp. Thoughtful minds on the kaiser's staff recognized their hubris. Russia's collapse "had been a boon of immeasurable value to us and should have been exploited to release troops for the West," Admiral Müller noted. Instead, Hindenburg and Ludendorff "conquered Latvia and Estonia and became involved with Finland—the results of an excess of megalomania." In supplanting civilian statesmen and Foreign Service professionals, Hindenburg and Ludendorff perpetrated "acts of violence" against the German people, Müller confessed to his diary.[6]

Throughout these negotiations Hindenburg remained steady—and this was both his virtue and his failing. His consistent message to soldiers and civilians alike was that victory was certain as long as they held their nerve. He reduced both combat and political negotiations to a contest of wills in which military considerations took priority over political ones, exactly the reverse of Bismarck's and Clausewitz's teachings. Unlike Foch or Haig, Hindenburg and Ludendorff showed no capacity for growth. Refusing to negotiate even from a position of strength, they persisted in dictating terms to enemies, allies, even their own countrymen. But implacable statesmen like Britain's David Lloyd George or France's Georges Clemenceau (known for good reason as "The Tiger") were not to be browbeaten or dictated to, especially with hundreds of thousands of American soldiers steaming across the Atlantic to bolster Entente defenses.

Hindenburg and Ludendorff now had to find a way to defeat Entente forces in the west. They had to allow enough time to redeploy nearly forty divisions from the eastern front to the west while launching the decisive offensive before American reinforcements deployed in large numbers. They also had to strengthen the will of a home front suffering through another difficult and fractious winter. Even Hindenburg and Ludendorff could not dismiss the munitions workers' strike of late January during which a million workers called for democratization and a nonannexationist peace without indemnities. A great military victory would silence these treasonous rabble-rousers and, in Ludendorff's telling phrase, stop them from devouring the marrow of the army.[7]

To silence agitators at home and enemies abroad, Hindenburg and Ludendorff placed their trust in battle. With Hindenburg providing political cover and moral stiffening, Ludendorff fleshed out an operational plan based on tactical virtuosity on the battlefield. No one questioned Ludendorff's technical skill, but his grip on strategy was tenuous. His plan, such as it was, constituted a desperate gamble for a larger Tannenberg attained through higher levels of frontline effectiveness. Short-term superiority in operational art, however, was not enough to overcome the long-term effects of the Entente's naval blockade and the bigger battalions of fresh troops arriving daily from the United States.

Here again, German strategy failed to relate means to ends. Hindenburg and Ludendorff simply lacked the means in 1918 to conduct a war-winning offensive in the west, but their minds admitted no other course of action. All will be solved once we pierce a hole, Ludendorff claimed. But this was not Prussia fighting Austria in 1866 or France in 1870. Instead, it was empires fighting empires, coalitions of nations fighting other coalitions. Ironically, panic created within the Entente by early German successes only drove Entente countries to cooperate more closely.

In the weeks of planning leading up to the great push, however, optimism surged both in the ranks and at higher headquarters. Speaking of one last trial of strength, Hindenburg again reduced complex geostrategy to a tug-of-war. In his preattack exhortation, he manfully asserted, "I am convinced that we will win. Where the will is, the way is also found. So forward with God!" Yet, God did not always march with German soldiers, despite what soldiers' belt buckles said.[8]

Codenamed Michael, the great *Kaiserschlacht* surged forward on March 21. Sixty-three German divisions flung themselves against the Arras–St. Quentin sector in the direction of the Somme and Amiens. After hurricane bombardments rained high explosives, shrapnel, and multiple types of poison gas on British positions, specially trained storm troopers in gas masks emerged like goggle-eyed insects from the dense mist and dust that shrouded the battlefield. The British Fifth Army under General Sir Hubert Gough, still recovering from the previous year's bloodletting at Passchendaele, reeled and then fled in confusion. At day's end German forces had advanced more than four miles, inflicting twenty thousand casualties on the BEF while bagging a further thirty thousand prisoners.

Ecstatic at this initial success, the kaiser pulled Hindenburg aside and pinned on his chest a military decoration theretofore unique in Prussian annals: the Iron Cross with Golden Rays. Only the great Marshal Blücher had been so decorated for his crushing victory over Napoleon in 1815. Ludendorff settled for the Iron Cross with Swords and Palms and the satisfaction that came with knowing that he had planned the assault. So confident was the kaiser that he was heard to declare, "The battle [is] won, the English utterly defeated."[9]

Hindenburg, however, remained unconvinced of victory and unmoved by his latest honor. "What is the use of all these orders?" he asked his wife. "A good and advantageous peace is what I should prefer. It is not my fault in any case if the struggle ends unfavorably for us."[10] His disavowal of responsibility was a disturbing harbinger of the *Dolchstoß* legend to come.

As German forces pushed forward, Ludendorff directed their

advances so as to develop and widen a gap near Amiens between the British and French armies. After splitting their enemies, German forces would then wheel northwards and drive the BEF into the sea. The thought also occurred to Haig and Pétain, who finally accepted the wisdom of a unified Entente command. At the Doullens conference on March 26, Ferdinand Foch was appointed generalissimo of Entente forces with the authority to shift reserves as needed to stem the German offensive. Foch's energy and optimism helped both to dispel paralysis at Haig's headquarters and to disperse the gloom pervading Pétain's headquarters. Meanwhile, Operation Michael slowed as Ludendorff diverted reinforcements in an ill-advised attempt to seize Arras.

As storm troopers consolidated territorial gains, they were both surprised and delighted to discover stashes of fine food, tobacco, wine, and whisky. Such luxuries were to them long forgotten. No less disconcerting were the mountains of uniforms, shoes, and underwear; the tins of bully beef and plum-and-apple jam at which British prisoners turned up their noses. German propaganda had spoken of Entente soldiers deprived even of basic necessities due to the U-boat campaign; clearly, the results of unrestricted submarine warfare had been exaggerated. Pausing to loot, German units also began meeting stiffer resistance. Their own fatigue and casualties slowed them as well.

Second-line infantry moved up to reinforce the assault, but their tactics were not as sound as those used by storm troopers. Less experienced, they tended to clump together in dense columns, providing both easy and significant targets for Entente artillery. Despite advancing up to forty miles and seizing twelve hundred square miles of territory, German forces failed to capture Amiens, the key rail center serving the British and French armies. Instead of being split, Anglo-French forces cooperated and restored their defensive cordon. Hindenburg especially praised the French for their timely counterattacks and skillful use of artillery that combined to weaken Germany's offensive strength. Altogether the Entente suffered nearly two hundred sixty thousand killed, wounded, or captured. German losses were of similar magnitude.

After Operation Michael's failure, Hindenburg and Ludendorff should have recognized that total victory by feats of arms was unattainable. But a military ethos that gloried in any challenge, no matter how daunting, drove them to persist in bludgeoning Entente lines. They mounted four more costly offensives from April to July in vain attempts to shatter the Entente's will. It was a case of *wir siegen uns zu Tode*, of the German military conquering itself to death.

As casualties continued to mount, the Ludendorff Offensives became a mincing machine. More disturbingly, the hecatombs of bodies were neither legitimated nor sanctified by tangible, war-winning results. Having already reached peak strength in mid-1917, the German army in 1918 grew ever weaker as it ground itself down in costly attacks. Impressive tactical successes were little more than skilful exercises in Verdun-like attrition, but it was the German army that was exhausting its last reserves.

Whereas the Entente by necessity had weaned itself from the cult of the offensive, Hindenburg and Ludendorff persisted in attacking, even as the material balance shifted against them. Rather than admit failure, Ludendorff lost himself in reassuring detail. By planning new offensives, he suppressed his own doubts but raised doubts within the army. Meanwhile, a relieved Foch, witnessing how Ludendorff continued to shift the focus of his attacks, mused, *Je me demande si Ludendorff connaît son métier.* Foch was not the only soldier at that time to question whether Ludendorff knew his craft.[11]

German forces could break into Entente defenses, sometimes they could break through, but they could never break out. In part this was due to material and technical limitations. The German army had only thirty-six thousand trucks, one third of the number available to Entente forces. Shortages of petrol and reliance on wooden- or iron-wheeled tires restricted mobility. Prone to break down in combat, trucks did not constitute an arm of exploitation.

Tanks may have provided breakout mobility, but Germany had only ten tanks available early in 1918, compared to eight hundred tanks available to Britain and France. Admittedly, tanks still lacked durability in combat due to their thin armor, poor reliability, and a cross-country speed little faster than that of an unburdened soldier walking. Germany's lack of tanks, however, was attributable not to technical immaturity but to a conscious decision on Hindenburg and Ludendorff's part to deemphasize machine warfare. "It is always bad," Hindenburg opined, "when an army tries, through technical innovation, to find a substitute for the spirit. That is irreplaceable."[12] But it was not an either-or choice. Tanks reinforced the spirit of Entente soldiers while instilling fear in the hardiest of German soldiers.

Possessing just a handful of tanks, the German army relied on the infantry for exploitation. But infantry advances could be held up for precious hours by a few well-placed machine gun posts. At the sharp end of battle, against automatic machine guns, rapid-firing rifles, and shrapnel bursts deadly to soldiers caught in the open, the German infantryman had only the speed of his two feet and the protection of a fraction of an inch of cloth. Shell-blasted terrain, looting, and simple exhaustion also slowed advances. Meanwhile, artillery had to be redeployed forward for fire support, a time-consuming but nevertheless essential task.

After Operation Michael's failure, Ludendorff pressed ahead on April 9 with the Lys Offensive (Operation Georgette). Again the focus was on British positions south of Ypres with the channel ports as the ultimate goal. Again, British lines bent but refused to break under the strain. Haig's forces, their backs to the wall, were aided by reinforcements coordinated by Foch. They held despite high losses. German forces suffered dearly as well, which precipitated an audacious move by a celebrated general staff officer.

Worrying that his counterparts at OHL were editing his dispatches before they reached Hindenburg and Ludendorff, Colonel Albrecht von Thaer journeyed to headquarters at

Avesnes in early May to report in person. Hindenburg listened silently to Thaer's description of frontline exhaustion and weakening morale but dismissed it as localized. Most other reports he received, Hindenburg reassured Thaer, spoke of "very good" and even "splendid" morale. Comforting Thaer, Hindenburg told him that the climate of OHL would soon mend his frayed nerves. Thaer's audience with Ludendorff was even more unsettling. Ludendorff dismissed as "prattle" Thaer's description of weakening morale and the poor quality of replacement soldiers. The army needed tougher commanders, Ludendorff concluded, not changes in strategy.[13]

By this time Hindenburg and Ludendorff were *frontfremd* (strangers to the front). Even worse, they tolerated and reinforced a climate that inhibited bad news from being relayed from frontline units to commanders at headquarters. Willful blindness led them to persist in launching yet another attack, the Aisne Offensive (Operation Blücher). It sought to divert French reserves from the British sector by attacking the Chemin des Dames ridge toward the Marne River. Launched on May 27, German forces caught the French Sixth Army deployed too far forward and pummeled it with artillery. Exposed to withering fire, French forces lost their cohesion and retreated in disorder.

For the first time since 1914, German forces raced toward and crossed the Marne River. Forgetting that the goal was to divert French reserves from the north, after which Germany could once again renew the assault in Flanders to drive British forces into the sea, Ludendorff exploited the French retreat by mounting a drive on Paris. But the bill for the renewal of unrestricted submarine warfare now came due. In their first large-scale engagement, the American Expeditionary Forces (AEF) under General John "Black Jack" Pershing blocked the German advance forty miles outside Paris at Château-Thierry and Belleau Wood. Once again, Germany was stymied.

Undeterred, Ludendorff mounted the Noyon/Montdidier Offensive on June 9. Lacking the element of surprise, this offensive gained only six miles as French resistance stiffened and German exhaustion set in. At this point Richard von Kühlmann, the state foreign secretary, made the reasonable suggestion that Germany should consider opening negotiations with the Entente. With considerable bile, Hindenburg and Ludendorff demanded his dismissal for promoting defeatism. Admiral Paul von Hintze, a staunch conservative, replaced Kühlmann.

Ludendorff launched the fifth and final drive, the Champagne/Marne Offensive, which he unwisely named *Friedensturm* (peace offensive), on July 15 with Paris as its goal. Well aware that an attack was coming, the French Fourth Army blunted the assault, ably assisted by the Italian corps at Dormans. In what became known as the second battle of the Marne, Entente forces, after three days of heavy fighting, pushed German forces back across the Marne River.

On paper, Germany's territorial gains in Ludendorff's five offensives looked impressive. But in launching these attacks, the Germans vacated fortified defensive zones along the Hindenburg Line. Their reward was three large salients that were vulnerable to flanking attacks. The front was also seventy-five miles longer and defended by fewer men of generally lower quality. (The German army suffered nearly a million casualties from March to July; Entente losses were similar but were made good by American reinforcements.) Meanwhile, by July the influenza epidemic, or "Spanish flu," infected half a million German soldiers, further weakening morale and overtaxing the medical services. Even more soldiers were infected by doubts about their leaders and the chances of ultimate victory. Doubt led to widespread shirking of duty. That summer, so many German soldiers took to hiding in attics and cellars to avoid returning to the front that local police forces were forced to turn a blind eye to them.[14]

What had gone wrong with the German war machine? Put simply, Hindenburg and Ludendorff pursued tactical/operational instead of strategic/political options for defeating the Entente. The former approach admitted rational solutions by diligent soldier-specialists; the latter approach required collaboration with allies and statesmen, both of whom Hindenburg and

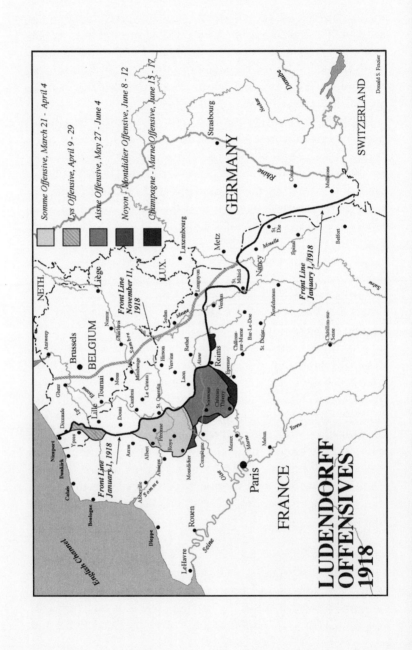

Somme Offensive, March 21 - April 4

Lys Offensive, April 9 - 29

Aisne Offensive, May 27 - June 4

Noyon - Montdidier Offensive, June 8 - 12

Champagne - Marne Offensive, June 15 - 17

Donald S. Frazier

SWITZERLAND

GERMANY

Rhine

Danube

Neckar

Strasbourg

Mulhouse

St. Dié

Colmar

Belfort

Épinal

Nancy

Moselle

Metz

Front Line January 1, 1918

LUXEMBOURG

LUX.

Longuyon

St. Mihiel

Verdun

Neufchateau

Saône

Chatillon-sur-Seine

St. Dizier

Bar-le-Duc

Châlons-sur-Marne

Épernay

Reims

Meuse

Sedan

Rethel

Aisne

Laon

Front Line November 11, 1918

NETH.

Liège

Namur

Charleroi

Sambre

BELGIUM

Brussels

Antwerp

Ghent

Tournai

Mons

Maubeuge

Hirson

Vervins

La Capelle

St. Quentin

Le Cateau

Cambrai

Douai

Lille

Lys

Dixmude

Nieuport

Dunkirk

Calais

Boulogne

English Channel

Dieppe

LeHavre

Rouen

Seine

Arras

Albert

Amiens

Somme

Péronne

Roye

Montdidier

Compiègne

Oise

Meaux

Marne

Melun

PARIS

FRANCE

Château-Thierry

Soissons

Front Line January 1, 1918

Yonne

Ypres

Abbeville

# LUDENDORFF
# OFFENSIVES
# 1918

Ludendorff held in contempt. Dismissing the inconstant and ir-resolute Emperor Karl of Austria-Hungary and the "babble building" of the Reichstag, OHL embraced battle with an intox-icating warrior spirit. Mounting offensive after offensive was the way to impose a superior Teutonic will on allies and enemies alike, or so it seemed to the duumvirate. Tactical and operational excellence, however, could not conceal, and in fact contributed to, underlying strategic rot.

Germany's successful strategy on the western front in 1917 had relied on elastic defense, featuring mutually supporting strong points and well-timed counterattacks by well-rested reserve divi-sions. In July 1918, Germany's defensive positions lacked depth, reserves, and supporting artillery. They were also vulnerable to flanking attacks. Hindenburg and Ludendorff recognized the problem but did nothing to solve it. Any withdrawal from terri-tory gained in the previous four months, they believed, would be an admission of failure with serious political consequences. Their paralysis condemned the German army to a slow and painful death.

Like Adolf Hitler's gamble at the Battle of the Bulge (Decem-ber 1944), Hindenburg and Ludendorff had committed the best of their remaining units in a desperate attempt at a military breakthrough. When their gamble failed, they dug in their heels and refused to budge, trusting in the resoluteness of the German army. It was now Foch's turn to play the role of Ulysses S. Grant to Hindenburg and Ludendorff's Robert E. Lee. Foch recog-nized that by shifting assaults along an attenuated German front, Hindenburg and Ludendorff would be forced to commit whatever reserves remained. As the duumvirate attempted to stem breaches in the line, superior Entente firepower, especially artillery, inflicted a heavy toll on German reinforcements as they moved in the open.

In retrospect, Foch's counteroffensive at the Marne salient on July 18 turned the tide in the Entente's favor. Backed by three hundred fifty tanks, it chewed up ten German divisions, mark-ing the end of Ludendorff's offensive striking power. From July

18 to November 11 Germany lost another four hundred twenty thousand men killed and three hundred forty thousand wounded or taken prisoner, all in a lost cause.[15]

Foch's breakthrough attack at the Marne provoked a crisis between Hindenburg and Ludendorff. As Ludendorff paced at the midday conference, Hindenburg suggested a major German counterattack against the left flank of Foch's assault. Taken aback by the field marshal's hands-on participation in operational decisions, Ludendorff muttered the idea was "utterly unfeasible." That night, Hindenburg repeated his suggestion. Several staff officers heard Ludendorff dismiss the idea as "nonsense." Hindenburg coolly replied, "I should like a word with you," with both men disappearing into Ludendorff's private study. The field marshal then reminded his second to remember his place.

This incident constituted an astonishing breakdown in discipline on Ludendorff's part. He had dared to ridicule the idea of his commander—the chief of the imperial general staff and a man eighteen years his senior. He never fully recovered from this crisis of confidence. After this, in Correlli Barnett's memorable description, "Ludendorff was like a beetle on its back, waving and wriggling furiously to no effect."[16]

In the coming months, the French army, BEF, and AEF sustained high losses but nevertheless kept unrelenting pressure on increasingly demoralized German forces. Throughout the summer of 1918, German soldiers and civilians alike repeatedly asked themselves why they continued to make sacrifices. An increasing number could no longer find answers. That summer's collapse of morale, blamed after the war on traitorous elements at the home front, was actually attributable to the betrayal of the cause for which German soldiers and sailors fought. And the betrayers were Hindenburg and Ludendorff. They continued to push their men to endure unsustainable losses in a lost cause. Told that spring that they were launching a "peace offensive," soldiers justifiably felt betrayed as fighting continued to rage with no conceivable victory in sight.[17]

As American troops continued to disembark at French ports at a rate of a division every two days, reaching three hundred thousand soldiers per month in July and August, German soldiers found themselves outnumbered, outgunned, and overmatched. Foch's coordinated attacks all along the front, supported by hundreds of tanks, airplanes, and profligate expenditure of artillery shells, led to breakdowns in German resistance.

Back at OHL, Ludendorff retreated into details, badgering subordinates with nitpicking questions. Meanwhile, Hindenburg seemed just as concerned with getting the details of various celebratory paintings right as he was in rescuing Germany's military position. Hindenburg had once declared that "the war suits me like a visit to a health resort." The irony here is that OHL was located at Spa, a Belgian health resort. Never once in mortal danger, too well insulated from *Frontsoldaten*, Hindenburg became detached, even callous. He refused to face the reality that disillusioned German citizens desired only release from perpetual war and their government's dominance of their lives.

Yet, perhaps "disillusion" does not quite capture the depths to which German morale had sunk. A better word might be *Zerrissenheit*, which conveys profound disorientation, dissonance, and despair.[18] In this climate, emotive words like *Vaterland* or *Heldentod* (hero's death) lost their meaning. As patriotic Germans struggled to make sense of their blasted mental landscape, they were vulnerable to soothingly simplistic propaganda. Far easier to believe a big lie—that radical socialists and war profiteers (especially of Jewish extraction) had betrayed Germany—than to accept the disturbing truth that Germany's betrayers were its most renowned and respected leaders.

The "Black Day of the German Army" (Ludendorff's description) came at Amiens on August 8, 1918. On this day, 604 Entente tanks tore a twenty-mile hole in the German defenses, through which "fast" (8 mph) Whippet tanks and armored cars, cavalry, and infantry poured. The sheer magnitude, pace, and shock of the blow drove German forces back eight miles; in their retreat, German forces shed thirty thousand men and four hundred guns. Retreating *Frontsoldaten* greeted reinforcements with bitter cries of "Blacklegs" (strike breakers) and "war-prolongers."

Ludendorff, shaken to the core by large-scale revolt within the army, issued a frantic call for an armistice—not to end the war, but to obtain breathing space so that German forces might regroup. Six days later, however, he and Hindenburg recovered their composure before the Crown Council. Enjoying the restorative surroundings of the ironically named Grand Hôtel Britannique at Spa, Hindenburg exuded strength and steadiness. The army could still enforce its will through staunch defense, he insisted. Hindenburg's optimism and understated resolve, attributes that had served him well at Tannenberg in 1914, now doomed the German army. Before Germany could hazard requesting an armistice, the army needed a face-saving victory, Hindenburg concluded. It seems not to have occurred to him, however, that the Entente also wanted to negotiate from a position of strength and would be loath to discuss terms on the heels of a German victory.

Hindenburg had little sense either of the mood of civilians or the war weariness of the army. Ensconced at Spa and kept well supplied with luxuries, he lacked firsthand knowledge of the deprivations endured by *Volk* and *Soldaten* alike. Germany had long passed the culminating point between offensive and defensive, victory and defeat, but Hindenburg remained oblivious. His misguided optimism did, however, cheer the Crown Council, which decided to deny Hertling the authority to pursue a diplomatic settlement.

Forced back to the Hindenburg Line in September, the German army lacked reserves to hold it. Entente forces showed they had learned from Germany's example. Preceded by intense and accurate hurricane bombardments using high explosives and poison gas, infantry attacks now came with little warning, used infiltration tactics similar to those developed by Germany's storm troopers, and were supported by tanks, aircraft, and well-timed creeping barrages. In a daring assault at Canal de St. Quentin on September 29, 1918, the French First Army, aided by the British Third and Fourth armies, pierced the Hindenburg Line.

That same week Ludendorff himself collapsed under the pressure.[19] Compounding bad news from the western front was the Entente's breakthrough at Salonika on September 15 and Bulgaria's fall on September 30. As Ludendorff raged for an immediate armistice regardless of the consequences, Hindenburg yet again attempted to restore calm. He even suggested that Germany might yet retain the iron ore fields in Briey and Longwy in occupied France! For once Ludendorff saw clearly, however, dismissing the field marshal's optimism as the purest fantasy.

As a psychiatrist reported to OHL to calm Ludendorff, the duumvirate looked for scapegoats. Ludendorff settled on socialists and other fifth columnists who sought a nonannexationist peace and who therefore sapped the people's will. "Let them now eat the broth they have cooked for us," he grumbled. While working to shift the blame, Ludendorff convinced Hindenburg and the Crown Council to issue a note on October 1 calling "for an immediate offer of peace" to "spare useless sacrifices for the German people and their allies."[20] But Entente leaders, recalling Germany's oppressive demands of Russia and Rumania, were unwilling to negotiate lenient terms now that the German army seemed on the verge of collapsing.

Having insisted all along that civilian leaders were merely along for the ride, Hindenburg and Ludendorff now demanded that they grab the reins and negotiate an immediate end to the war. Hindenburg himself confessed to the Crown Council on October 2 that "there appears to be no possibility . . . of winning peace from our enemies by force of arms."[21] Rather than blaming the home front, Hindenburg accurately cited the inexorable wearing down of the army in encounters with fresh forces being fielded by the Entente.[22]

That same day Reichstag leaders were finally informed that the duumvirate was seeking an immediate armistice to forestall a collapse of the army. Caught unawares, the Reichstag dissolved in bitter recriminations. Rudderless without a chancellor (Hertling had resigned at the end of September), the Reichstag and Crown Council settled on Prince Max, heir to the grand duchy of Baden. A distant cousin of the kaiser, Prince Max had previously issued calls for peace negotiations. Sworn in as chancellor on October 3, he began forming a government along more democratic lines.

Events now began to accelerate. Prince Max quickly contacted President Wilson to request an armistice on the basis of the Fourteen Points. He soon discovered that Entente demands had grown since January. Three quick exchanges took place. At each exchange, Wilson, spurred on by Entente leaders, grew more determined to punish Germany.

After the second exchange, the German War Cabinet met in Berlin on October 17 to discuss strategy. Despite having convinced the kaiser on September 29 that Germany needed an armistice, Hindenburg and Ludendorff now called for continued military resistance. Having stared defeat in the face and blinked, the duumvirate nevertheless refused to accept their and Germany's ultimate fate. It was a combination of being unwilling to conceive of the inconceivable—that the army had failed the test of war—and a cynical effort to shift blame from themselves to Germany's new civilian leaders. Ludendorff even flirted with the notion of an *Endkampf*, an apocalyptic last stand on German soil, based on a levy of anyone left standing and able to pull a trigger. Sentiment for a final battle in defense of the fatherland, originating among conservatives and radical nationalists, extended rapidly, though briefly, into the cosmopolitan elites of Berlin and the left-center parties of the Reichstag before foundering on the shoals of military reality.[23]

In his third note, dated October 23, Wilson refused to negotiate further as long as the kaiser, his fellow "monarchical autocrats," and his "military masters" remained in control. Wilson also insisted that Germany capitulate, not just agree to an armistice that could be used for breathing space. This and other demands were too bitter a pill for Hindenburg and Ludendorff to swallow. The next day they proclaimed in an Order of the Day that Wilson's latest terms were "unacceptable" to "us soldiers at the front" since they would leave Germany defenseless. The conceit here is apparent. Having no recent, firsthand knowledge of frontline conditions and widespread discontent within the ranks, Hindenburg and Ludendorff still thought it possible that the army would fight to the last man.[24]

But the German army was a skeleton of its former self. Its dispirited soldiers no longer believed in the heroes of Tannenberg. A popular riddle that sped from trench to trench that fall asked, "Why are Hindenburg and Ludendorff like the Sun?" The reply, "Because they rise in the east and set in the west," provoked pained and humorless smiles. (The German word, *untergehen*, meaning "set," also connotes decline.)

Trying to salvage what was left of imperial Germany, Prince Max demanded that Hindenburg and Ludendorff disavow their proclamation. Stubbornly, they refused. Denouncing them as insolent and insubordinate, Prince Max went to the kaiser to submit his own resignation. Faced with the resignation of the chancellor and his cabinet, the kaiser finally grasped the nettle. He summoned Hindenburg and Ludendorff to appear before him. On October 26, Ludendorff again submitted his resignation; this time, the kaiser willingly accepted it. In Hindenburg's presence Ludendorff took his leave. Hindenburg haltingly and halfheartedly offered his own resignation, but the kaiser demurred, recognizing that the field marshal's heroic stature was needed now more than ever if a complete collapse of army discipline was to be averted.

As Hindenburg left the kaiser's residence, he found Ludendorff glowering outside. The latter assumed that if he had been cashiered, then so had Hindenburg. Upon learning that Hindenburg still served, Ludendorff snapped, accusing him of treating him shabbily. He then refused to ride in the same car with Hindenburg back to headquarters. Although shocked by Ludendorff's impertinence and ingratitude, Hindenburg dutifully returned to their common office and mourned the professional death of "a particularly dear friend."[25] Thus ended the tumultuous four-year "marriage" of the victors of Tannenberg.

Upon hearing that the kaiser had at last accepted Ludendorff's resignation, Prince Max and his staff jumped to their feet, crying "Thank God." All were pleased that Hindenburg remained. Showing the shrewdness that got him to the top, Hindenburg left the armistice negotiations to the new government, thus granting the army and OHL plausible deniability. Germany's chief representative for armistice negotiations, Matthias Erzberger, was head of the Catholic Center Party.[26] Junior officers represented the army and navy (a major general and a captain, respectively). Hindenburg was more than happy to leave "these unfortunate [armistice] negotiations" at Compiègne to civilians and midlevel military men.

The brush of total defeat, therefore, tarred Germany's nascent parliamentary government instead of the army. This was no accident. By the summer of 1918, Pan-Germans had already laid the foundation for the *Dolchstoß* myth, even identifying the guilty party. In a harrowing statement, the chairman of the Pan-German League declared on October 19 that Germany's impending collapse "should be used for a fanfare against Jewry and the Jews as lightning conductors for all injustices."[27] While fully embracing the *Dolchstoß*, Hindenburg toned down its anti-Semitic virulence. Nazi leaders would show no such compunction.

The mutiny of Germany's High Seas Fleet at Kiel on November 4 soon spread throughout the navy as well as much of the army. Faced with the need of informing the kaiser that the army no longer stood behind him, Hindenburg first defended his emperor, then was struck dumb. To the Old Prussian Hindenburg, his oath of loyalty to the kaiser truly was unbreakable. The unenviable chore then fell to General Groener, a Swabian and Ludendorff's replacement as first quartermaster general. After surveying Germany's senior army commanders, Groener told the kaiser on November 9 that the army no longer obeyed its emperor's commands.[28] Wilhelm turned in desperation to Hindenburg, who could only nod his head in silent confirmation of the truth of Groener's statement.

Here again, in his hesitant, yet dignified, way, Hindenburg played a key role. As Wilhelm concocted mad schemes of seeking an alliance with Britain against the United States, Hindenburg's sober mien and mantle of authority forced him back to reality. The kaiser knew Hindenburg was an avowed monarchist. When even the field marshal agreed that the imperial crown was untenable, Wilhelm knew his reign was over. As he tearfully relinquished one crown, Wilhelm clung desperately to the crown of Prussia. Smothering this last gasp was Prince Max's declaration that the kaiser had renounced both crowns. (The dissipated and unpopular Crown Prince Willy also renounced his right to succession.) Prince Max then resigned his position as chancellor, turning it over to Friedrich Ebert, leader of the majority Socialist Party.

Facing a Spartacist revolt that included the seizure of the imperial palace, Ebert knew he needed the army's support to quell charismatic radicals like Karl Liebknecht (who after his release from prison was carried on the shoulders of hardened combat veterans). Acting quickly, Groener engineered a deal with Hindenburg. Telephoning Ebert, Groener offered the army's support in putting down the revolutionary workers' and soldiers' councils. In return, he asked Ebert to support the army within the new republic. Clinching the deal for Ebert was Hindenburg's willingness to remain at his post to oversee the peaceful return and demobilization of the imperial army.

Truly a shadow monarch now, the ex-kaiser for his own safety sought exile in the Netherlands as the Reichstag declared that a republic existed in Germany. It was a republic without republicans, however. The overriding question was whether a socialist "revolution from above" was sufficient to forestall a Bolshevik revolution from below. The answer hinged on the loyalty and strength of those elements of the army that survived demobilization; they soon proved both willing and able to crush radical workers' and soldiers' councils.

The German army's moral and physical collapse in 1918 invites comparison to the French army's mutiny in 1917. Leaders of both armies had pushed their men beyond the point of endurance. German commanders, however, were unable to produce the comprehensive "remobilization" based on renegotiation of "working conditions" that kept France in the war until the arrival of the Yanks and the tanks.[29] By November the OHL could count no more than a dozen divisions as able and willing to fight. Clearly, the fish had rotted from its head; Hindenburg and Ludendorff had betrayed the trust of the army and of the German people.

Why had the Entente prevailed? Besides blundering into the bloody and tedious, but ultimately winning, combination of attrition warfare on land and economic warfare at sea, the Entente demonstrated, with the rise of Lloyd George and Clemenceau, the value of civilian control over policy and diplomacy. They followed Clausewitz far better than did Hindenburg and Ludendorff. As the young Charles de Gaulle noted, the duumvirate forced "the capitulation of the civil power to military authority, which was now without a counterweight." Lacking a counterweight, Hindenburg and Ludendorff embraced and enforced their own peculiar brand of German militarism: "the characteristic taste for immoderate undertakings; the passion to expand their personal power at any cost; the contempt for the limits marked out by human experience, common sense, and the law."[30]

The Entente also waged coalition warfare more effectively than did Germany. While distrust plagued both sides, France and Britain found a way to work toward the same end, unlike Germany and Austria-Hungary, who fought uncoordinated campaigns on different fronts against different enemies. As the war continued, Germany found itself expending vital resources to sustain an ally that stubbornly refused to trim its behavior and pretensions to its diminishing capacities. Austrian generals, moreover, joined their German overlords both in failing to profit from Russia's collapse in 1917 and in turning a blind eye to signs of rising disaffection within the ranks. With military exhaustion came the dissolution of two dynasties—Hohenzollern and Hapsburg—whose subjects came to loathe their rulers even more than they feared their enemies.

In contrast to the Central powers, the Entente used a wider array of strategic means in pursuit of their ends. Especially skilled in their use of propaganda were the British, who used it both to strengthen resolve at home and to convince the United States to aid the Entente. Germany, in contrast, unwisely dismissed America's military potential and inflamed public opinion with the Zimmermann telegram and U-boat attacks. More clearly than the Central powers, the Entente recognized the wider dimensions of grand strategy. Battles were only one means to victory and not always the most important when compared with political, economic, intellectual, and psychological means. The genius, or, more accurately, the operational proficiency, of Hindenburg, Ludendorff, and the German military was evident but insufficient. The Entente suffered higher casualties on the battlefield but used a wider array of means under firmer political control to erode Germany's will.

Paradoxically, whereas Ludendorff soon became a fringe figure on the extreme right and eventually an embarrassment even to the Nazis, Hindenburg's reputation survived Germany's collapse largely intact. Despite losing the war and betraying his oath to the kaiser, Hindenburg avoided blame. The icon of German militarism proved amazingly resilient—a testament to Hindenburg's gravitas, as well as the German people's need for a noble figure who could uphold the nation's dignity in defeat.

The apparent suddenness of the collapse, however, gave Germans little time to adjust. Memories soon proved malleable. Exhausted and disaffected *Frontsoldaten* came to suppress or forget their leaders' betrayal. Instead, many waxed nostalgic for the sense of purpose the war had given them and the lost comradeship of the trenches. A minority sought to rekindle the flame of German militarism. An emotionally shattered Adolf Hitler was only the most famous example.

Not all German soldiers forgot, however. In 1924 General

Freiherr von Schoenaich bluntly wrote that "we owe our ruin to the supremacy of our military authorities over civilian authorities; and that is the very essence of militarism. In fact, German militarism simply committed suicide."[31] Humiliation at Versailles, political turmoil, and hyperinflation in the early 1920s, however, encouraged many Germans to look again to a strong man to provide honor, stability, and direction. In 1925 Germany again called Hindenburg out of retirement, with a result even more catastrophic for Germany and the world.

# Weimar and Hitler

A S THREE MILLION German soldiers straggled back from the front, abandoning the hard-won gains of more than four years of combat, Germany devolved into street fighting between left wing activists and rightist elements. Concerns about a successful Bolshevik revolution in Germany occupied the minds of Entente representatives. Foch and his compatriots nevertheless pressed ahead with tough armistice terms that November. Under these terms, Germany had to evacuate Belgium, Luxembourg, France, and Alsace-Lorraine within two weeks; evacuate the Rhineland within a month, including a ten-kilometer zone along the east bank of the Rhine river; evacuate Russia, Rumania, and Italy; turn over five thousand locomotives and one hundred fifty thousand rail cars to the Entente in two weeks (thereby denying strategic mobility to the German army); and release all Entente prisoners of war (POWs). Meanwhile, the Entente asserted its right to hold German POWs until Germany signed the final peace treaty and kept the naval blockade in place as well. Germans continued to starve in thousands as the fledgling republic debated whether to sign the Versailles Treaty or renew the fight.

By remaining at his post and overseeing the demobilization of the army, Hindenburg provided an invaluable service to the Council of People's Deputies (soon to become the Weimar Republic). His mere presence was enough to prevent a military coup. Furthermore, he lent his support to aggressive efforts to stamp out Bolshevism. The Spartacist uprising in Berlin in January 1919, led by Karl Liebknecht and Rosa Luxemburg, was brutally suppressed, with both Liebknecht and Luxemburg murdered while in police custody. In March, Bolshevik uprisings were again suppressed with the help of *Freikorps,* irregular rightist military units, as the bodies of revolutionaries and unlucky bystanders caught in the crossfire littered Munich's streets. Ruthless action against the radical Left gave the Weimar Republic the breathing space it needed to consolidate control over postwar Germany.

In forming a parliamentary republic whose constitution supported universal suffrage and proportional representation, Weimar Germany challenged and defeated long odds. In eastern Europe, struggles between agrarian land reform parties and the reactionary old order saw the triumph of right-wing strongmen, whether in Admiral Miklós Horthy's Hungary or General Józef Pitsudski's Poland. These dictatorships evolved into the fascist regimes of the later 1920s and 1930s. Under *Reichspräsident* Ebert's leadership, the fledgling Weimar Republic averted, at least for the time being, military takeover and fascist dictatorship.

Yet, Hindenburg and the military's cooperation came at a high price. Hindenburg was allowed to wash his hands of treaty negotiations, forcing Weimar's civilian leadership to affix their names to the Versailles Treaty, finally signed on June 28, 1919. Before acquiescing to the signing, Hindenburg considered renewing the war, writing that "as a soldier I cannot help feeling that it were better to perish honorably than accept a disgraceful peace." Concluding that effective military resistance was impossible, he once again turned to Groener, who conveyed the harsh reality to the government. Yet, even token resistance may have discour-

aged a burgeoning *im Felde unbesiegt* myth—a sentiment engraved on numerous war memorials across Germany—that the
German army had remained unvanquished in battle.

The Versailles Treaty reduced a once-dominant imperial army
of four million to one hundred thousand and eliminated the
general staff, its nerve center. Cadet schools were closed. Other
terms gutted the navy and abolished the air force. Under Article
231, the infamous war-shame clause, Germany and its allies had
to admit culpability as the aggressors, thereby justifying debilitating war reparations. Entente forces were to occupy the
Rhineland for fifteen years, after which the region was to be demilitarized forever. These terms, demanding as they were, represented a compromise with even tougher terms proposed by the
French. Foch advocated Germany's evisceration—a return to the
pre-1871 structure of independent and competitive Germanic
states—to prevent a future resurgence. Overruled by Wilson and
Lloyd George, Foch declared that the so-called peace of Versailles was merely a twenty-year armistice—certainly one of the
most prophetic statements ever made.[1]

The Paris Peace Conference strangled the nascent Weimar
Republic in the cradle. Article 231's black-and-white vision of
war culpability provoked widespread outrage in Germany and
generated sympathy for its war veterans. The tragedy here is that
General John Pershing, among others, had warned that leaving
the German army intact without its experiencing the humiliation of a final defeat would delude Germany into thinking it had
been perfidiously sold out rather than physically whipped. Instead of destroying the German army in battle, the war-weary
Entente punished Weimar, subverting confidence in it while
abetting the German military's efforts to deflect blame from its
leaders.[2]

The Versailles Treaty had two key flaws: The Entente powers
lacked the will to enforce its strictest terms, yet the latter were
highlighted and exploited by reactionary elements in Germany,
who referred to the treaty as a *Diktat,* or dictated peace. Millions
of grieving Germans, believing they had fought a just war in a

just cause, concurred. So did Hindenburg. And so did a demo-
bilized *Gefreiter* (private first class), of Austrian birth but a decorated veteran of the Bavarian army, soon to discover latent
rhetorical and political skills in Munich's beer halls.[3]

After overseeing the army's orderly return, as well as evading
responsibility for the Versailles *Diktat*, Hindenburg retired in
July 1919 from active military service, this time for good. That
August, during the fifth anniversary of Tannenberg, he urged
German youth "not to lose the spirit of the great age" of Moltke
the Elder despite the distractions of this "meek and spineless"
time. Thus, it was an unwise parliament that called an unrepen-
tant field marshal to the stand later that November to testify as
to the reasons for Germany's defeat in the war. Hindenburg had
recently renewed his partnership with Ludendorff, now back
from self-imposed exile in Sweden. Ludendorff helped prepare
his chief for his testimony before the parliamentary committee.
As an exercise in myth making and self-absolution, Hindenburg's testimony would soon rank "among the most politically
effective words ever uttered."[4]

In a dramatic display of imperiousness, Hindenburg ignored
the question put to him as to the thought process and timing of
Germany's decision to renew unrestricted submarine warfare. In
a prepared statement, he instead absolved the German army of
responsibility for having lost the war. Citing an anonymous
British general,[5] Hindenburg declared that disloyal elements on
the home front had stabbed the army in the back, just as Hagen's
treacherous spear had slain noble Siegfried. In the tumult that
followed, an unbowed Hindenburg imposed his will on a chas-
tened assembly.

Put charitably, Hindenburg emerged here a slave to his Prussian prejudices and preconceptions. Inability to take responsibility for Germany's collapse in 1918 was his fatal flaw, albeit a
predictable one. His undiminished status as Germany's greatest
war hero ensured that the *Dolchstoßlegende* was broadcast
throughout Germany. Like many myths, it had a sliver of truth
to it. Had not many Germans failed to give their last full meas-

Cadet Hindenburg, Berlin, 1865. *Author's collection.*

Lieutenant Hindenburg as adjutant of the Third Regiment of Foot Guards during the Franco-Prussian War, 1870–1871. *Author's collection.*

Captain Hindenburg of the general staff, Stettin, 1878.
*Author's collection.*

Colonel Hindenburg, commander of the Ninety-First
Infantry Regiment, Oldenburg, 1894. *Author's collection.*

General Hindenburg, chief of staff of the Eighth Army Corps, Coblenz, 1897. *Author's collection.*

Patriotic postcard from World War I featuring the heroes of Tannenberg, Field Marshal Hindenburg (right), and his chief of staff Ludendorff (left). *Author's collection.*

Painting of the field marshal from a 1915 postcard. Hindenburg is wearing his dress uniform with plumed hat and sword. His right hand clutches his field marshal's baton, a symbol of rank and prestige not only in the imperial army but also in its successor, Hitler's Wehrmacht. *Author's collection.*

Propaganda postcard depicting Hindenburg scooping up Russians at the second battle of the Masurian Lakes, 1915. *Author's collection.*

Aufgenommen von Ihrer Majestät der Kaiserin und Königin im Juli 1915

Rotophot A. G. Berlin.

Hindenburg with the kaiser (left) in 1915. Note how Wilhelm II hides his withered left arm. *Author's collection.*

Unsere Führer: Hindenburg und Hötzendorf.

Painting of Hindenburg with his nominal ally, Austrian chief of the general staff Conrad von Hötzendorf. *Author's collection.*

The ersatz kaiser, Hindenburg (left), and *der Feldwebel,* Ludendorff (right), flank Kaiser Wilhelm in 1918. Hindenburg wears his special Iron Cross with Golden Rays on his left breast. *Library of Congress.*

The field marshal on the hunt and enjoying his retirement in 1923. *Author's collection.*

PRESENTING THE NEW PRESIDENT OF GERMANY

U.S. political cartoon after the German presidential election of 1925. Which was the döppelganger? *Library of Congress.*

Discharging presidential duties. *Author's collection.*

Hindenburg looks askance at the "Bohemian Corporal," now chancellor of Germany, January 1933. *USAF Academy, Special Collections.*

Hitler, at podium, oversees Hindenburg's interment at the Tannenberg Memorial, 1934. One wonders what the pious field marshal would have thought of Hitler's pagan exhortation, "And now enter into Valhalla!" *USAF Academy, Special Collections.*

ure to the war effort? Might they not now feel pangs of guilt and acquiesce in the myth that it was not the veterans who had served so honorably but they, their neighbors, and especially marginal elements in society who were truly the guilty parties?

The stab-in-the-back mantra proved persuasive precisely because the German people wanted to deflect blame from frontline veterans to disorderly or disreputable elements in civil society. These elements included Bolsheviks, profiteers, and other "unpatriotic" groups. Despite their considerable sacrifices in the war, German Jews soon found themselves in that category as well, mainly due to their association in wide circles of gentile opinion with big business, high finance, and socialism, no matter that the first two and the last were mutually exclusive. In an intellectual matrix increasingly penetrated by pseudoscientific racial theories, German Jews came to be seen as the worst of the conspirators who had betrayed a country that had nurtured them richly. The *Dolchstoßlegende* quickly became a leading theme of Nazi propaganda.

For Hindenburg personally, the myth freed him from blame. Instead of taking responsibility for defeat, Hindenburg spoke of collective unworthiness.[6] More disturbingly, a murderous and, at times, even criminal war acquired a sheen of Nordic nobility and tragedy. The truth was that much of the German army had lost its moral bearings in the war. Colonel General Karl von Einem, commander of the Third Army, confessed in 1918 that his soldiers had become a "gang of thieves," adding that, "*One* motive for the bravery of our infantry . . . is the lust for plunder."[7] The criminalization of the army reflected the brutalization of German society.[8] Collective indiscipline—a breakdown in *Zusammengehörigkeitsgefühl,* or the sense of belonging within units—was then covered up by a mendacious exercise in self-serving myth making.[9]

Foch was right to dismiss Ludendorff as a mere soldier but wrong to praise Hindenburg as a patriot.[10] Ludendorff embodied militarism gone mad, a Moloch who demanded more and more of his men until war consumed them. Yet, Hindenburg exhibited the patriotism of self-interest. Certainly, he loved Prussia, possessed a strong, if selective, sense of honor (he offered himself to the Entente in place of the kaiser), and wanted little more than the kaiser's restoration. At the same time, he was unwilling to work sincerely for a republican Germany. Instead, he fought tenacious rearguard actions against political democracy and the decline of the landed elite. In the process, he allowed himself to be co-opted by rightist elements and, eventually, by Hitler, through bribes, flattery, and promises of a return to glory for the army.

Prone to narcissism, Hindenburg toiled to secure his legacy. For a land-poor Prussian like himself that included reclaiming and then enlarging the family's ancestral estate at Neudeck. In 1927 the government (of which he was then president) granted Neudeck to him, funded by a national collection and grants from wealthy industrialists and landowners.[11] After he chose Hitler as chancellor in 1933, the latter enlarged Neudeck with a tax-free grant of an additional five thousand acres. Hindenburg may have been the first military man whom Hitler bribed into silent complicity.[12]

But the catastrophe of Hitler's rise to power still lay in the future. During his second retirement from July 1919 to March 1925, Hindenburg hunted, expanded his kitschy collection of Madonna-and-child artwork, and basked in the warm glow of the near universal adulation of his countrymen. The death of his wife in May 1921 marked the most trying event for him. Her passing left Hindenburg bereft and alone. She was his sounding board; she knew him as a husband and father, not as an icon. The balance and companionship she provided he would sorely miss. If she had lived, one wonders if she could have dissuaded him from answering what he considered his final call to duty as president in 1925.

The year 1923 marked the end game of Weimar's violent consolidation. As French forces occupied the Ruhr valley in an attempt to compel Germany to pay its reparations, the German government adopted a deliberate policy of hyperinflation that destroyed the savings of the middle class. Economic chaos led to the radicalization of politics and the abortive Nazi coup in Munich led by Ludendorff and Hitler. Hitler, sentenced to five years in prison, served nine months. To his chagrin, Ludendorff was released on personal recognizance. Thus, he was available in August 1924 for the tenth anniversary of the Battle of Tannenberg. At Hohenstein the battle's victors (minus Hoffmann, who was ill) gathered for the laying of the foundation stone of a grandiose memorial. Striking the stone three times, Hindenburg dedicated the memorial to the fallen, to the living, and to future generations. More than one hundred thousand Germans witnessed this solemn ceremony.

Under the steady hand of Gustav Stresemann, a nationalist who briefly served as chancellor in 1923 and as foreign minister thereafter, and propped up by loans from the United States and a rescheduled plan for reparations (the Dawes Plan), Germany made a strong recovery. By early 1925, political stability and economic prosperity reduced radical parties such as Hitler's National Socialist German Workers' Party (NSDAP) to nuisances (the Nazis gained less than 3 percent of the parliamentary vote in 1924 and 1928). Ebert's unexpected death in February, however, threatened to derail the recovery. With the republic's first presidential election scheduled in March, Catholics and liberals united behind a single candidate, Center Party leader Wilhelm Marx. A former chancellor, Marx was colorless but competent. Rightist and Protestant parties cast about for a rival candidate amenable to a similar broad range of interest groups. Unexpectedly, they converged on Hindenburg.

Unlike 1914, however, the field marshal was reluctant to answer the call. This was politics, not a military command, and Hindenburg at first declined to run. But a visit from Tirpitz changed his mind. Speaking man to man, the cagey, fork-bearded admiral appealed to Hindenburg's vanity (which was considerable) and his sense of duty (which was self-defined but all-encompassing). He made vague, yet compelling, references to Hindenburg's potential ability as president to push Germany back in the direction of monarchy. The chance to serve his country—and possibly to re-store the kaiser—overpowered Hindenburg's distaste for politics.

Hindenburg tried to remain above the political fray, but many workers and even some veterans refused to sanction his candidacy. A typical attack from the left went as follows:

> Vote for the Mass-Murderer?
> Vote for the Kaiser's Henchman?
> Vote for the Profiteer's Friend?
> Vote for the Hangman of Democracy?
> If you would elect all four
> VOTE FOR HINDENBURG!![13]

Amplifying the attack was Theodor Lessing. A German Jew who swung from total assimilation to Zionism, Lessing wrote an essay that dismissed Hindenburg as a "zero" whose reign would set the stage for a "future Nero." For these harsh yet prescient words, Lessing was later forced to flee in 1933 to Czechoslovakia, where Nazi thugs tracked him down and murdered him at Marienbad on August 31, 1933.

In a close election, Hindenburg won a simple majority and the presidency on April 26, 1925. He was now the caretaker of Europe's most dynamic and aggrieved country. Ludendorff, meanwhile, was caught in his own private maelstrom, railing about an unlikely worldwide conspiracy involving Jews, Jesuits, and Freemasons. Recognizing he could no longer afford to associate with Ludendorff's fantasies, Hindenburg wrote to the scribbling conspiracy theorist that presidential duties prevented him from making his annual visit to Ludendorff's home. As in October 1918, Ludendorff exploded in anger. He never spoke favorably of Hindenburg again.

Another critic was Harry Kessler. Known as the "Red Count" for his pacifism and republican sympathies, Kessler derided Hindenburg as "the god of all those who long for a return to philistinism and the glorious time when it was only necessary to make money and accompany a decent digestion with a pious upward glance." His election, Kessler concluded, constituted a "farewell"

EUROPE 1924

New Nations

SWEDEN

FINLAND

Helsinki

NORWAY

Revel

ESTONIA

LATVIA

Riga

Moscow

IRISH
FREE
STATE

GREAT
BRITAIN

Dublin

LITHUANIA

Kaunas

SOVIET
UNION

Danzig

NETH.

East
Prussia

London

Berlin

Warsaw

BELG.

GERMANY

POLAND

Rhineland

Prague

Paris

Alsace-
Lorraine

CZECHOSLOVAKIA

Vienna

Budapest

SWITZ.

AUSTRIA

HUNGARY

RUMANIA

FRANCE

Bucharest

ITALY

Belgrade

YUGOSLAVIA

PORT.

Rome

BULGARIA

Sofia

ALBANIA

Ankara

SPAIN

GREECE

TURKEY

Athens

both to progress and a "vision of a new world which was to be humanity's conscience money for the criminal war."[14]

But for most Germans, Hindenburg's election represented a return to normalcy. After the calamity of World War I and the revolutionary strife of the early 1920s, boring politics were a relief. In Europe and America visionary leaders like David Lloyd George or Woodrow Wilson were rejected. Their replacements, men like Austen Chamberlain, Warren G. Harding, and "Silent Cal" Coolidge, were staid, humdrum leaders. Lloyd George himself approved of the German people's selection of "a very sensible old man."[15] People needed time to mourn their dead and reflect or, alternatively, to celebrate survival and escape from painful memories. Craving stability and national unity, Germans rallied behind Hindenburg as an ersatz kaiser and father to a "fatherless generation."[16] As long as domestic politics remained stable, Hindenburg stayed the course, keeping above party intrigue and petty interest groups and providing continuity between old and new.

In the symbolic aspects of the presidency, Hindenburg excelled. Among his first official duties was leading the delegation to rebury Manfred von Richthofen, the Red Baron, in German soil at the Invaliden Cemetery. Dressed in his field marshal's uniform, Germany's oldest living hero honored one of Germany's younger and most dashing fallen heroes. Soon Richthofen's grave became a shrine for young Germans seeking a resurgence of Teutonic vigor.

Donning his field marshal's uniform again, Hindenburg also presided over army group command maneuvers in September 1926. Journalists enthused about a "new wave" rolling over Germany, a resurgent respect and even love of the army. In the town of Mergentheim, "Hundreds of people jammed the streets in front of Hindenburg's hotel, serenading the old man with the *Deutschlandlied*, weeping, holding up their infants to catch a glimpse of him."[17] Just as Hindenburg had in 1888 hoisted young Oskar to see Wilhelm I lying in state, now other German parents were raising their children to the new president and substitute kaiser.

Even more memorably, Hindenburg presided over the dedication in August 1927 of the Tannenberg Memorial. Consisting of eight towers connected by a massive wall, the Stonehenge-like amphitheater enfolded up to ten thousand "worshippers" in mystic solidarity. The "sacred site" incorporated the tombs of twenty unknown soldiers who had perished on the eastern front. Hindenburg seized this opportunity, on behalf of "the whole German nation in every walk of life," to repudiate the "war-guilt" clause of the Versailles Treaty.[18] Marring the dedication was Ludendorff's refusal to stand at Hindenburg's side.[19] Ostracism by his colleagues was Ludendorff's reward. In their headlong retreat in 1945, *Wehrmacht* engineers destroyed the memorial rather than risk its desecration by advancing Soviet units.

As Hindenburg traveled across Germany, giving speeches and accepting honors, he followed a policy of strict constitutionalism that did him credit. Most notably, he supported Stresemann in the fall of 1925 during sensitive negotiations with France and Great Britain. Under the resultant Treaty of Locarno, Germany recognized the permanence of its postwar boundaries in the west. In return, France and Britain left open the possibility of renegotiated boundaries for Germany in the east.[20] Germany was then considered for and admitted to the League of Nations in September 1926 with a permanent seat on the council. Nationalists criticized Hindenburg for supporting Stresemann's policy of constructive engagement. Weathering the storm, he emerged even stronger, more of a central figure than before.

Two scandals marred his first term as president. The first involved General Hans von Seeckt, successor to Hindenburg as head of the army's high command. Seeckt led the *Reichswehr* as a force representing and defending the republic, although he left it to others to suppress right-wing putsches like those of Kapp and Hitler.[21] Seeckt's undoing was to invite the grandson of the exiled kaiser to participate in the army's annual maneuvers. As president, Hindenburg ultimately commanded the army and navy. Sympathetic to Seeckt's monarchism but alienated by his arrogance, Hindenburg dismissed him. The controversy bore the trademark of Kurt von Schleicher, an ambitious colonel and confidant of Oskar, Hindenburg's son.[22] With Oskar now serving as his father's aide, a coterie of ambitious manipulators began coalescing around Hindenburg *père et fils* (father and son). For the time being, Otto Meissner, secretary of state and Hindenburg's most trusted factotum, kept them at arm's length.

The second scandal involved the *Junkers,* or landed aristocracy, and had two elements. The first involved a proposal to refuse public reimbursement of princely holdings confiscated after the revolution, which Hindenburg opposed successfully but not without compromising his oath to stay above factional politics. The second involved the *Osthilfe,* or eastern aid, a fund established to help large landowners meet their debts. Three hundred thousand marks were earmarked for this fund, but many landowners abused their loans, dissipating the money on gambling, prostitutes, and other pleasures. The scandal was suppressed, but not before the Nazis got wind of it. They later used threats of its exposure as a lever to pry open the door to the chancellery.

But the *Vater des Volkes* (father of the people) celebrated his eightieth birthday on October 2, 1927, free of the taint of scandal. As commemorative coins and stamps bearing his image circulated in the millions, Hindenburg was showered with gifts and honored with speeches. A typical encomium came from one Dr. Guenther-Holstein. "When the German people elected Hindenburg," intoned the good doctor, "it admitted the morality of its whole history, admitted in particular the morality of its war, which it had waged with the whole of the heavy, ethical seriousness that is characteristic of the Germans."[23] On this day, Hindenburg sounded the depths of Germany's collective soul. If he had died before 1930, he might be remembered today as one of Germany's greatest leaders. However, it was not he but Stresemann who died just prior to the onset of the Great Depression. Economic dislocation, together with an increasingly antirepublican shift in Weimar's landscape (as seen in Alfred Hugenberg's takeover of the German National People's Party in 1928), soon radicalized German politics and ravaged the prosperity and stability so painstakingly engineered over the previous five years.

Originating in the United States in 1929, the Great Depression deepened and spread throughout Europe in 1930. As American banks called in their short-term loans, Austrian and German banks failed. Businesses collapsed and factories closed their doors, throwing large numbers of Germans out of work and terrifying most of the rest. Germany's chancellor, Hermann Müller, saw his grand coalition of socialists and centrists collapse in March 1930 over the issue of unemployment compensation to workers. As centrists argued for fiscal austerity and cuts in unemployment benefits to balance the budget, socialists took the side of workers and withdrew from the government. Hindenburg's tendency to evade responsibility, his reactionary instincts, and his impatience with less-than-tractable political problems now combined to spell Weimar's undoing. Aging, perturbed, and increasingly overwhelmed by events, he allowed himself to be manipulated by a palace camarilla consisting of von Schleicher (now a general), Meissner, Franz von Papen, and his son, Oskar.

Schleicher, originator of the *Freikorps* and a polished political general, persuaded Hindenburg to appoint Heinrich Brüning as chancellor. A distinguished combat veteran, devoted Catholic, and shrewd politician, Brüning pushed through an economic austerity program. After the Reichstag rejected it, Hindenburg implemented the policy by emergency decree, an ostensibly time-limited power granted to him under Article 48 of the constitution. As no government could command a parliamentary majority, Hindenburg found himself becoming a protoführer, ruling Germany from 1930 to early 1933 by emergency decrees. (In 1932 he issued sixty-six decrees, whereas the Reichstag succeeded in passing only five laws.) Brüning proceeded to dissolve the Reichstag. In new elections held that September, Hitler's NSDAP surged from 12 to 107 seats to become the second-largest party after the socialists in the Reichstag.

As unemployment rates soared, Nazi slogans promising action captured the attention of a disoriented and discontented voting public that feared a return to the lawlessness and penury characteristic of 1923. Hitler and the NSDAP's message was simple. It called for a reversal of the Versailles *Diktat,* followed by ambitious and (most likely) bloody efforts to secure "living space" in the east for racially superior Aryans; for the suppression of communists (who had also gained followers as unemployment rates rose); and (ominously) for revenge against the "November criminals." Nazi thugs—the *Sturmabteilung* (SA or Brownshirts)—took to the streets, blustering, bristling, and beating home their anti-Semitic, anti-Marxist, and antiliberal screed.

They were helped by the *Reichswehr's* growing willingness to accept the Nazi movement as the army's civilian counterpart, as a national body above and outside the everyday give-and-take of politics, and correspondingly representative of Germany's general will. Lengthy terms of service—commissioned officers served a minimum of twenty-five years, enlisted soldiers for twelve years—reinforced the army's identity as a separate state within the state, one that republican virtues rarely penetrated.[24] Like their presidential commander in chief, the *Reichswehr's* senior officers were predominately monarchists. The junior ranks were less nostalgic but shared a general dislike of *die ungeliebte Republik* (the unloved republic). Officers internalized an ethic of professionalism, combining Prussian attitudes with a longing for the modern weaponry of which Versailles deprived them; they remained predominately aristocratic, although there were a few bourgeois bounders like Erwin Rommel. Embracing a vitalistic theory of war that extolled moral factors and spirit, *Reichswehr* intellectuals found Nazism compelling. Many officers found Hitler himself vulgar and distasteful but nevertheless sympathized with the NSDAP's brash militarism and fervid nationalism. Dynamic, confident, aggressive, Nazism also respected and promoted more mundane soldierly virtues like discipline, courage, and comradeship.

Senior officers in the *Reichswehr* wanted neither to suppress
the brawling Brownshirts nor to send them home. Rather, they
wanted to see them in army *Feldgrau* (field gray uniforms). By
incorporating the enthusiasm of the Nazis into the framework of
the army, officers like Schleicher hoped to restore Germany's position in central Europe in a series of limited wars against opponents intimidated by memories of World War I. They soon
discovered that Hitler had far more ambitious designs than
merely restoring Germany's position in Europe.

In seeking to co-opt the army, the Nazis were unafraid to attack Hindenburg as passé. In 1930 Joseph Goebbels published a
cartoon depicting the field marshal as a pitiless Teutonic god
watching impassively as German workers were led away in
chains (a reference to the Young Plan, which restructured but
still enforced Germany's schedule of war reparations). Suing for
libel, Hindenburg won the case. Goebbels escaped with a token
fine of eight hundred marks and free publicity that implied the
NSDAP, not Hindenburg, was the more reliable ally of workers.[25]

As the Nazis continued to win supporters, especially among
the young, Hindenburg grew increasingly uneasy. Brüning, attacked as the "Hunger Chancellor" for his fiscal conservatism,
remained in power but earned no new friends as he made new
enemies. His seven-year presidential term set to expire in 1932,
Hindenburg wanted little more than to retire for a third and final time. But retiring was out of the question when his chief op-
ponent was Hitler. That spring, aided by the unlikely support of
a center–left coalition who saw him as the only viable alternative
to Hitler, Hindenburg on the second ballot secured a majority of
53 percent of the vote to Hitler's 37 percent. Hindenburg was
president for a second seven-year term, although few thought he
would live long enough to finish it. Nevertheless, Hindenburg's
alleged quip that Hitler's next position would be as a postmaster
licking the backs of stamps bearing the president's image still
seemed apropos.[26]

Emboldened by Hitler's setback, Brüning persuaded Hindenburg to issue a decree banning the SA and Heinrich Himmler's *Schutzstaffel* (SS), or Blackshirts. It lasted less than a week. The *Reichswehr*, in the person of Schleicher, fatefully intervened and persuaded Hindenburg to lift the ban (Schleicher still planned to use the SA and SS to rebuild Germany's military strength). Meanwhile, Brüning's half measures and unpopularity led to his dismissal as chancellor at the end of May. His replacement, Franz von Papen, less skilled as a statesman than he was as a horseman and raconteur, was a favorite of Hindenburg (the president called him "Fränzchen," an affectionate diminutive). Papen gathered a bland group of likeminded conservative ministers around him (known derisively as the "cabinet of barons") who conspired with Hindenburg to tear down what was left of the unloved republic. With Hindenburg's blessing, Papen ordered a military takeover of the legal government of Prussia, whose socialist and centrist nature was an affront to conservatives. General Gerd von Rundstedt handled the action with dispatch on July 20, 1932.

That same month, Schleicher colluded with Hitler for new parliamentary elections. The NSDAP gained another 123 seats in the Reichstag to attain a plurality. But could Hitler translate electoral success into the chancellorship? No one knew for sure. Relations between Hindenburg and Hitler had always been strained. The field marshal treated the "Bohemian Corporal" with loosely veiled contempt. To Hindenburg, Hitler was an upstart and untrustworthy rabble-rouser. For his part, Hitler saw Hindenburg as a broken-down has-been, but remained deferential in public settings. It is possible, as Konrad Heiden has speculated, that Hindenburg reminded Hitler of the domineering father he had feared and detested—the same square head, the florid mustache, the gruff and critical demeanor.[27]

Like Alois Hitler, Hindenburg found little about Adolf to like and even less to respect. He called him to the carpet in a historic meeting that August. Standing unconfidently before the field marshal, Hitler defended his decision not to support the Papen government. Instead, Hitler mumbled that he deserved the dominant role in it, "like Benito Mussolini in Italy." Irritated by Hitler's impudence, Hindenburg chastised him for failing to do his duty to the fatherland. He further warned him he would "counter with all severity" the violent hooliganism of the Brownshirts. A government announcement followed that made it clear Hitler had overstepped his bounds. Even worse, the announcement implied he had gone back on his word to the president. A furious Hitler refused to countenance a coup, deciding instead to force the issue by engineering a vote of no confidence against Papen's government. With 512 deputies voting against and only 42 voting for, Papen was forced to dissolve the Reichstag. In new elections held in November, the NSDAP lost thirty-four seats but remained the largest party. The Papen "cabinet of barons," lacking popular support, twisted in the wind and soon snapped.

Earlier in September, the British ambassador had noted that "the old field-marshal is the only fixed point in the present state of flux" but that this fact "perhaps constitutes the most serious feature of the political situation" in Germany. And the "indispensable" Hindenburg was at wit's end.[28] Twenty governments had come and gone in the thirteen years of Weimar's existence. As the Nazis whispered about the *Osthilfe* scandal and the president's complicity therein, Papen overplayed his hand and sought wider powers from Hindenburg. On December 2, 1932, Hindenburg acted, dismissing Papen and naming Schleicher chancellor. Papen still remained a favorite, however, receiving from Hindenburg an autographed card that read, "I had a comrade."[29] It was more thanks than Brüning had received and also more than Schleicher would receive. For, like Papen, Schleicher failed to mobilize popular support, then sought extraconstitutional powers, powers that Hindenburg was still loath to grant.

It is often said that Hindenburg had begun to show signs of senility, but if he had, his opposition to Hitler remained uncompromised. The president, however, was worn down and fed up; his eighty-five years weighed heavily upon him. Itself under stress, his camarilla now betrayed him. Recognizing his momentum was in danger of stalling, Hitler gambled everything and won. On January 4, 1933, he met secretly with Papen and agreed to become chancellor with only two other Nazis in the cabinet: Wilhelm Frick as minister of the interior and Göring as minister without portfolio (but Göring also seconded Papen as minister of the interior for Prussia). Capturing the interior ministries of Germany and Prussia meant that the Nazis would control the police, augmented by their own private army of SA and SS. In an attempt to restrict Hitler's influence, Papen would serve as vice chancellor and accompany Hitler to his audiences with Hindenburg, who preferred not to address Hitler directly.

Advised by Papen, Meissner, and most importantly by his son, Oskar, who had met secretly with Hitler on January 22, that Hitler would be brought to heel and humbled within a nationalist cabinet, a dilatory and depressed Hindenburg acquiesced. "We have hired him!" Papen exclaimed as a new cabinet was formed with Hitler as chancellor.[30] Not for the first time, those in authority had underestimated Hitler. Hindenburg was hardly alone in misjudging the man,[31] but only he could legally appoint Hitler, and history has not allowed him to evade responsibility.

Historians, however, have been less successful in explaining his decision. The most familiar argument presents Hindenburg as an aged, exhausted pawn in the hands of Papen, the right-wing camarilla, and not least Oskar. To the extent he remained an independent actor—and there is ample evidence that his vigor waxed and waned in these final days—Hindenburg may have been influenced by the argument that the Nazis' loss of votes in the November 1932 election would make them easier to handle. On a more visceral level, it is likely that Hindenburg preferred a Nazi government to continued disorder and trusted his conservative cronies to keep Hitler in line. A united, vigorous, and nationalist Germany under Hitler's direction was better than the all-too-likely result of attempting to govern without him and his enthusiastic followers. Cabinets made and unmade by cabals with no visible bases of public support made for a political situation that could not endure indefinitely. A war game held in late November 1932 concluded that the *Reichswehr* and

the Prussian police together could not put down a civil war engineered by the Nazis and communists. The consequence of
such a war, to a monarchist and conservative like Hindenburg,
would be the end of Prussia and the Germany he had spent his
life serving; the Reich's enemies, foreign and domestic, would
pick its bones.

Instead, as conservatives attempted to capture the dynamism
of the Nazi movement while curbing its criminality, the opposite
occurred: The Nazis co-opted their legitimacy and used it
brazenly in a sadistic reign of terror that consumed all political
rivals. Ironically, the man who saw Germany's future most
clearly at the end of January 1933 was Ludendorff. Having
marched alongside Hitler in the Munich putsch, Ludendorff
had no illusions about a new, law-abiding version. "This ac-
cursed man," Ludendorff telegrammed to Hindenburg, "will
cast our Reich into the abyss and bring our nation to inconceivable misery. Future generations will damn you in your grave for
what you have done."[32] So they would.

The announcement on January 30, 1933, of Hitler's appointment as chancellor touched off a frenzy of Nazi demonstrations,
including a torchlight parade that evening in Berlin. "It's like a
fairy tale," enthused Goebbels. From their respective offices
Hitler and Hindenburg watched the procession make its way
down the Wilhelmstraße. A story soon circulated that, if not literally true, was taken as symptomatic of Hindenburg's decline.
As thousands of SA and SS shuffled past, followed by the
Stahlhelm, or Steel Helmets, the nationalist war veterans' organization, in ringing cadence, Hindenburg reputedly beamed with
pride, then turned to an imaginary Ludendorff in the shadows
and exulted, "Ludendorff. How well our men are marching! And
what a lot of Russian prisoners they've taken!"[33]

Having finally attained power legally, Hitler moved to liqui-
date all rivals. The sheer pace of Nazi consolidation stunned
nearly everyone. Aiding them was a Decree for the Protection of
the German People issued by Hindenburg in early February,
which curtailed freedoms of assembly and the press. A key event

was the Reichstag fire of February 27, 1933. Started by Marinus van der Lubbe, a former Dutch communist, the fire provided a ready-made pretext for a crackdown. The fire, the Nazis falsely claimed, was a prearranged signal for a general communist uprising. Ostensibly to prevent civil war, Hindenburg issued yet another emergency decree outlawing the Communist Party and suspending regular judicial procedures. By April twenty five thousand people had been placed in "protective custody" (a euphemism for arbitrary arrest and indefinite imprisonment) in Prussia alone. Some of Hindenburg's erstwhile supporters found themselves locked up as enemies of the state. The situation was summed up in a joke that made the rounds in Berlin.

"Have you heard," a man would whisper to a trusted friend, "Hindenburg was at the Oranienburg Concentration Camp yesterday?"

"Why?" his friend would reply.

"He wanted to visit some of his electors."

"That's nothing. They say the old man signs anything now. The other day Meissner left his sandwich bag on the table and when he came back the president had signed it."[34]

Even in an atmosphere ripe with crisis and murderous intimidation, Hitler and the NSDAP failed to win a majority of the vote. In the last free elections to be held in Germany until 1946, the Nazis won 44 percent of the votes, necessitating a coalition government with the nationalists. Thus, in March 1933, 56 percent of the German electorate was still voting against Hitler. But it was also true that the German people granted him a large plurality, and nearly a majority, a vote of confidence that seemed to justify Hindenburg's selection of him as chancellor.

To strengthen his image as a legitimate, law-abiding leader, Hitler orchestrated a masterful ceremony on March 21, 1933, for his installation as chancellor. The location, the Garrison Church at Potsdam, was a shrine to the House of Hohenzollern. It contained the tombs of Frederick the Great and his father. In 1866 Hindenburg had stood here as a young lieutenant in the Third Foot Guards. Now, as he strode slowly up the aisle, arrayed in his dress uniform festooned with decorations and orders, he saluted the kaiser's empty throne with his field marshal's baton. It was an empty gesture. On this Day of Potsdam, it was not the field marshal restoring his imperial master to the throne, but the venerable *Reichspräsident* embracing the new *Reichskanzler*, embodying and representing the common soldier of the Great War. Hitler gave a masterful speech, praising Hindenburg for his "greathearted decision" that forged a new union of "old greatness" with "youthful strength." Shutters clicked as a deferential Hitler clasped the hand and bowed before the mighty field marshal.

This image of Hitler bowing before Hindenburg was tremendously influential. For the Nazis it meant respectability, legitimacy, and continuity with a martial past that translated into an ever-tightening grip on the *Reichswehr*. To opponents of Nazism in and outside Germany, it offered hope. The Viennese Jew George Clare recalled thinking, "How servilely Hitler bows before the ramrod old field marshal. How disdainfully that old soldier looks down on that little man . . . so ridiculously turned out in white tie and tails; like a head-waiter from Sacher's except that head-waiters at Sacher's had better-fitting clothes."[35]

The day prior to Potsdam, a German Jew, Victor Klemperer, saw more clearly. Having seen a recent newsreel of Hindenburg, Klemperer, himself no longer young, noted in his diary how the field marshal now walked with "the tiny, laborious steps of a cripple." His speeches were "laborious, his breath short, the voice of a very old man who is physically near the end."[36]

After the grand success of Potsdam, Hitler succeeded two days later in bullying the Reichstag to vote for the Enabling Act, effectively signing its own death certificate. Only the Social Democrats courageously voted against the act, ostensibly needed "to eliminate the distress of the nation and Reich." It did so by transferring power from the Reichstag to Hitler as chancellor, granting him near dictatorial powers for four years. Hindenburg, who by this time was in semiretirement at Neudeck, evidently saw it as a release from the burdens of his office. Four months later, the NSDAP was Germany's only legal party. The ever-astute Victor Klemperer noted in his diary how Goebbels now boasted of Hitler as the "absolute master" of Germany. Hindenburg was unmentioned.[37]

Moving against enemies, real and perceived, Hitler briefly ran afoul of Hindenburg one final time in April. As the Nazis began openly to persecute German Jews, Hindenburg objected to the dismissal from civil service of German-Jewish veterans wounded in the war. Such dismissals, Hindenburg wrote, were "wholly intolerable." If these men "were good enough to fight and shed their blood for Germany they should also be regarded as good enough to continue serving the Fatherland in their profession." Hitler replied ominously that "certain actions" would have to be concealed in the coming years and that therefore "untrustworthy elements" had to be removed now to gainsay state security for the future.[38]

Subverted by the Nazis, Hindenburg's entourage worked to interdict the flow of complaints submitted for presidential review. Thus, Hindenburg knew little of the extent to which the Nazis purged the civil service, established a police state, dominated the press and radio, and even supplanted the judiciary with their own parallel People's Tribunal system. The year 1933 also witnessed the creation of *Konzentrationslager* (concentration camps) such as Dachau for the incarceration of enemies of the state (in the early years, primarily communist sympathizers, pacifists, and other "resisters," with a smattering of real criminals, who ironically were treated better than the political prisoners). Even worse, the Nazis began their program of compulsory sterilization of the mentally ill, retarded, habitual criminals, and other "unfit" Germans.[39] Like a whitewashed sepulcher, Hitler and the Nazi regime hid behind a façade of law and order, a façade that always faced a fading president.

Hitler now faced only two internal rivals: the *Reichswehr* and his own unruly Brownshirts. By purging the latter, he cemented the support of the former. In the "Night of the Long Knives" on June 30, 1934, Hitler used the SS and Gestapo (secret police) to purge the SA. After its head and Hitler's old comrade, Ernst

Röhm, refused to shoot himself, the SS pulled the trigger for him. General Schleicher, the former chancellor, and his wife were gunned down in cold blood in their Berlin home. Gustav von Kahr, who had turned against Hitler's Munich putsch in 1923, was hacked to death. Pieces of his body turned up in a swamp near Dachau. Somebody sent a telegram under Hindenburg's signature thanking Hitler for his "resolute and courageous action."[40]

Mercifully for Hindenburg, a much more peaceful end for him was near. He died in the morning of August 2, 1934. With his death, the Nazis combined the office of president and chancellor into one person: Hitler. Hindenburg desired a simple grave next to his wife's at the family church at Neudeck. Yet, even in death he was not done playing a role in facilitating the Third Reich's rise. After a memorial session at the Reichstag that included the playing of Siegfried's Funeral March from *Götterdämmerung*, Hitler presided over an ostentatious state funeral for Hindenburg at the Tannenberg Memorial, where the field marshal's body was interred together with his wife's. "And now enter into Valhalla!" the Führer operatically concluded. Wotan may have applauded, but Hindenburg—a man of undemonstrative Protestant piety—would have cringed at Hitler's Wagnerian pretensions. The Nazis thoughtfully provided reading material for the afterlife by including copies of Hitler's *Mein Kampf*, Alfred Rosenberg's *Myth of the Twentieth Century* (an anti-Semitic diatribe), and Friedrich Nietzsche's *Thus Spake Zarathustra*.[41] With Hindenburg dead, the army was now free to swear an oath of allegiance to the Führer instead of to the constitution. Led by General Werner von Blomberg, a fervid Nazi, the new *Wehrmacht* did precisely that.[42]

In many German homes, depictions of Hindenburg remained as iconic representations of old Germany, joined by images of Hitler as the symbol of new Germany. Few people recognized how uneasily these images shared each other's company. In contesting for the soul of Germany, the icon of German militarism proved to be the lesser god; the cult of *der Führer* overwrote that of *der Alte Herr* (the old gentleman). For a complex set of reasons that may never be fully fathomed, a regime of unprecedented criminality and evil had arisen from the ashes of military collapse and economic despair. For his role in facilitating this vast human tragedy, Hindenburg has yet fully to receive the opprobrium he deserved.

# Epilogue

PAUL VON HINDENBURG reached maturity as the Second Reich emerged triumphantly from the Franco-Prussian War. As Germany sought to cohere as a nation-state in fin de siècle Europe while simultaneously reaching out for its own imperial place in the sun, the *Junker*-dominated officer corps in which Hindenburg proudly served provided the glue that enabled Wilhelm II to maintain a semiauthoritarian rule into the twentieth century. In return, Hindenburg and his brother officers earned the enviable status that came with serving in imperial Germany's most visible and admired institution, an army that had earned its spurs by producing decisive victories on the battlefield. Even professors were known to flaunt reserve commissions and when introduced, chose to have their military rank announced first, academic credentials second.

Hindenburg's retirement in 1911 marked a fitting end to a respectable military career. It certainly did not weaken the feudal bond he felt to his liege lord, the kaiser. Recalled to active duty in the opening weeks of the war, Hindenburg won acclaim and celebrity with impressive victories at Tannenberg and Masurian Lakes. With Ludendorff by his side, in two years Hindenburg rose from command of an army, to field marshal and overlord of Germany's eastern front, and eventually to chief of the imperial general staff. By 1917 these men became virtual military dictators of Germany, and by extension Austria-Hungary as well as Germany took over a faltering Hapsburg war effort.

Excessive power and near-universal adulation exposed Hindenburg's shortcomings. The wooden statues that became his wartime symbol unintentionally captured a certain woodenness of character. Strength and fortitude Hindenburg possessed; dexterity and breadth of vision he did not. Effective as an army commander, he was out of his depth as a coalition commander and especially as a soldier-statesman. Rejecting negotiated settlements to the war as dishonorable and pusillanimous, Hindenburg and Ludendorff agreed that all-out offensives in every sphere, military, political, and intellectual, were the answer. Unrestricted submarine warfare, however, failed and inexorably dragged the United States into the war, restoring the morale of faltering Entente forces. Meanwhile, overweening ambition in the east prevented concentration of force in the west. Bewilderment and strategic overstretch combined to produce all-or-nothing attacks on the western front from March to July 1918 that ended in exhaustion and widespread disillusionment on both the battlefront and the home front.

Together, Hindenburg and Ludendorff had failed to honor their promises to the soldiers wearing field gray, ultimately betraying their trust. Instead of taking their share of the blame, Hindenburg and Ludendorff sought scapegoats. Defeat marked an acrimonious split of the so-called marriage between these men. Recrimination and betrayal replaced cooperation and mutual respect. Their bitter divorce was a minor, if telling, manifestation of the totality of the Second Reich's moral collapse.

Precipitous collapse of German morale, together with the suddenness of the kaiser's abdication, profoundly shocked a nation that was still being told as late as October 1918 that it was winning the war. The next year saw Hindenburg at his finest and his worst. As the vindictive and increasingly vacuous Ludendorff railed in exile, Hindenburg stayed at his post, overseeing the orderly return of the German army, the violent suppression of revolutionary forces, and the reluctant conclusion of the Treaty of Versailles.

Yet, after months of commendable service, Hindenburg maliciously lent his iconic stature to the myth that *im Felde unbesiegt*, that on the field of battle the German army had remained unvanquished. Who, then, was responsible for the Second Reich's collapse and ultimate humiliation? Refusing to accept blame, Hindenburg testified in November 1919 to a *Dolchstoß* administered by conspirators and traitors at the home front. Images of betrayal resonated powerfully with disenchanted veterans and the families of those killed, reluctant as they were to accept that their sacrifices had ultimately been thrown away in a lost cause. Better to shift the blame to marginalized elements within society.[1] Such treachery seemed foreordained in the mythology of the *Nibelungenlied.* The Second Reich's demise was thus life imitating art, a Wagnerian tragedy in which heroic Siegfrieds had once again been stabbed in the back by scheming Hagens.

Not all Germans accepted the myth, of course. Yet, it proved easier for many soldiers and their families to attribute Germany's defeat to enemies within the body politic than to admit their own blame or to give proper credit to opponents without. His ring-leading role in propagating and perpetuating the *Dolchstoßlegende,* together with his reluctant role in acquiescing to Hitler's appointment as chancellor, transformed Hindenburg into a false icon.

As president of Weimar from 1925 to 1934, Hindenburg assumed a certain nobility as *Vater des Volkes* (father of the people) or, more affectionately, *der Alte Herr* (the old gentleman). At equal turns stolid and avuncular, gruff and grandfatherly, he helped to stabilize Weimar but also allowed himself to be *sich mit Wuerde schieben lassen* (shoved with dignity) by rightists. Tragically, he was the only leader who commanded enough respect from the people to prevent Hitler's election as president in 1932. In placing their trust in an eighty-five-year-old retired field marshal who had already sold his soul in November 1919, however, the German people played into the hands of right-wing militarists and fascist criminals.

The relationship between Hindenburg and the German people, a relationship built on shared illusions and dependencies as well as trust, even love, proved disastrous to both. During and after the war, the German people transformed Hindenburg into an icon. As such, he became an object of unremitting public interest and adulation. As a young boy, he had once asked for nothing more than peace and quiet. But his own legend, symbolized both by the titanic wooden statue in Berlin and by the thousands of mass-produced "Iron Hindenburgs" replicated in its image, icons that seemed to promise ultimate victory as long as worshipers remained steadfast, strong, and sure, made it impossible for him to secure peace and privacy.[2] Perhaps this is one reason he hunted so avidly: In the woods, he found a measure of peace and privacy. Otherwise, he was always on stage, always being studied and worshiped. Knowing this, he grew ever more jealous of his dignity, nobility, and legacy.

The mask of Olympian calm he wore began to wear thin, however, when events forced him to collaborate with the center–left to win reelection to the presidency in 1932. With a healthy push from his advisors, Hindenburg swung fatally back to the right, in part to efface the stain of having had to truck with socialists and other liberal elements. Haunted still by a sense of betrayal for his passive role in the kaiser's abdication in 1918, Hindenburg conspired with conservatives to end the Weimar experiment. The appointment of Hitler, he appears to have concluded, would serve as a way station on the road to monarchical restoration. Like previous chancellors, Hitler would be overcome by events and dismissed, even as more venerable nationalists tapped the NSDAP's popularity while moderating its more irrational and violent elements.

Many, perhaps most, Germans in 1933 craved both the decency and stability provided by Hindenburg and the decisiveness and dynamism promised by Hitler. "The stable decent majority of the German people," Winston Churchill noted, with their "ingrained love of massive and majestic authority, clung to [Hindenburg] till his dying gasp."[3] Yet, it would be wrong to view the ageing Hindenburg as a misguided figurehead who acquiesced under pressure in giving Hitler legitimacy. The reality was different and more damning. In Hitler's catastrophic rise Hindenburg was a witting accessory before the fact. By propagating the *Dolchstoßlegende* and investing it with all the authority and luster his heroic image could muster, Hindenburg sowed the seeds of more insidious deceptions. This icon of German militarism became a tin drum that the Nazis beat to entice a new generation of Germans to march to war. Embracing a lie, Hindenburg made a Faustian bargain to preserve his Old Prussian soul. The legacy of this lie was a criminal regime of unprecedented evil and a world in flames.

# Notes

*Preface*

1. "Bohemian" referred not only to Hitler's geographic origins, which Hindenburg apparently mistook as Braunau in Bohemia, but to the fact that Hitler's German incorporated the counterpart of a pronounced rural upper-southern twang, an intonation having the same visceral negative effect on many northern Germans and educated people as its U.S. counterpart. Thus, "Bohemian Corporal" was an understood euphemism for "hillbilly grunt."
2. S. Haffner, *Defying Hitler*, trans. Oliver Pretzel (New York: Farrar, Straus and Giroux, 2002), 7.

*Chapter 1: Prewar*

1. Paul von Hindenburg, *Out of My Life* (New York: Harper and Brothers, 1921), 1:6.
2. William C. Dreher, "Von Hindenburg, General and Man," in *History of the World War*, ed. Frank H. Simonds, 5 vols. (New York: Doubleday Page & Co., 1917–20), 2:391–405: on 394.
3. Helene Nostitz von Hindenburg, *Hindenburg at Home: An Intimate Biography* (New York: Duffield & Green, 1931), 30–31.
4. Dennis E. Showalter, *Railroads and Rifles: Soldiers, Technology, and the Unification of Germany* (Hamden, CT: Archon Books, 1976).
5. Dreher, "Von Hindenburg, General and Man," 394.
6. Rudolph Weterstetten and A. M. K. Watson, *The Biography of President von Hindenburg* (New York: The Macmillan Company, 1930), 12.
7. Hindenburg, *Out of My Life*, 1:46, 88.

8. Norman Stone, "Field-Marshal Paul von Hindenburg," in *The War Lords: Military Commanders of the Twentieth Century*, ed. Michael Carver (Boston: Little, Brown & Co., 1976), 46.

9. Hindenburg, *Out of My Life*, 1:76–77.

10. Hindenburg, *Out of My Life*, 1:80.

11. Weterstetten and Watson, *Hindenburg*, 32.

12. From 1904 to 1924 he shot 104 wild boar, 76 roebuck, 27 red deer, 24 does, 6 black cock, 6 chamois, and assorted minor game. During the war he also added a bison and elk to his wall of trophies. See Emil Ludwig, *Hindenburg* (Philadelphia: The John C. Winston Co., 1935), 73. He continued to hunt well into his eighties, shooting a trophy stag outside of Berlin while serving as president.

13. Hindenburg, *Out of My Life*, 1:89.

14. French leaders held similar convictions; Ferdinand Foch declared, "Victory is willpower."

15. Hindenburg was a great admirer of Scipio Africanus, a Roman general who sought to force and win battles of annihilation. See Nostitz von Hindenburg, *Hindenburg at Home*, 71.

*Chapter 2: The Eastern Front, 1914–1916*

1. Hindenburg quoted in Walter Görlitz, ed., *The Kaiser and His Court: The Diaries, Note Books and Letters of Admiral Georg Alexander von Müller, Chief of the Naval Cabinet, 1914–1918* (London: Macdonald & Co., 1961), 204.

2. Alfred Kelly, *The Descent of Darwin: The Popularization of Darwinism in Germany, 1860–1914* (Chapel Hill: University of North Carolina Press, 1981), shows how Darwinian concepts spread from elites to the masses.

3. Stig Förster, "Der deutsche Generalstab und die Illusion des kurzen Krieges, 1871–1914: Metakritik eines Mythos," *Militärgeschichtliche Mitteilungen* 54 (1995): 61–95, is a groundbreaking reinterpretation of the short-war issue in a German context. Also debunking the myth of universal war enthusiasm is Jeffrey Verhey, *The Spirit of 1914: Militarism, Myth, and Mobilization in Germany, 1914* (Cambridge: Cambridge University Press, 2000). Alternatively, MacGregor Knox suggests that the most seductive myth of "the August Days" was that of national integration, the belief that, with war upon them, the

German people finally put aside petty animosities to become one *Volk*. This myth helped inspire the founders of the Fatherland Party in 1917. See Knox, *Common Destiny: Dictatorship, Foreign Policy, and War in Fascist Italy and Nazi Germany* (Cambridge: Cambridge University Press, 2000). Hew Strachan provides an insightful overview of the mood of 1914 in *To Arms,* vol. 1 of *The First World War* (Oxford: Oxford University Press, 2001), ch. 2.

4. See the vignette in Alfred M. Knox, *With the Russian Army* (London, Hutchinson & Co., 1921), 1:123.

5. Erich Ludendorff, *Ludendorff's Own Story, August 1914–November 1918: The Great War from the Siege of Liège to the Signing of the Armistice as Viewed from the Grand Headquarters of the German Army,* 2 vols. (New York: Harper and Brothers, 1919), 1:14; Hindenburg, *Out of My Life,* 1:104–105.

6. For details see Dennis E. Showalter, *Tannenberg: Clash of Empires* (Hamden, CT: Archon, 1991; Dulles, VA: Brassey's, 2004).

7. Ludendorff and Hoffmann also claimed credit in their respective memoirs. Naming victory also has many fathers!

8. Hindenburg, *Out of My Life,* 1:123.

9. Ludwig, *Hindenburg,* 126.

10. Albert Speer recalled that each nail cost one mark. See his *Inside the Third Reich: Memoirs* (London: Book Club Associates, 1971), 52. Reproductions of the titanic wooden statue of Hindenburg in Berlin could be purchased in various sizes and materials. An advertisement for these modestly sized "Iron Hindenburgs" is reproduced in Jay Winter, *Sites of Memory, Sites of Mourning: The Great War in European Cultural History* (Cambridge: Cambridge University Press, 1995), 83.

11. Dennis E. Showalter, "From Deterrence to Doomsday Machine: The German Way of War, 1890–1914," *The Journal of Military History* 64 (2000): 679–710.

12. Dennis E. Showalter, "'The East Gives Nothing Back': The Great War and the German Army in Russia," *The Journal of the Historical Society* 2 (Winter 2002): 1–19.

13. Gary W. Shanafelt, *The Secret Enemy: Austria-Hungary and the German Alliance, 1914–1918* (New York: Columbia University Press, 1985); Holger H. Herwig, "Disjointed Allies: Coalition

Warfare in Berlin and Vienna, 1914," *The Journal of Military History* 54 (1990): 265–80.

14. Görlitz, *The Kaiser and His Court*, 47. Hindenburg often served as a "corset stay" for Ludendorff. For example, when Ludendorff began to panic during Haig's attack at Arras on April 9, 1917, Hindenburg put an arm around his shoulder, saying "We have lived through more critical times than this together." Hindenburg's ability to keep his head while others were losing theirs was a powerful force multiplier, to use modern military parlance.

15. Dreher, "Von Hindenburg, General and Man," 403.

16. *Helden* quickly became ubiquitous as a modifier, notes Robert Weldon Whalen in *Bitter Wounds: German Victims of the Great War, 1914–1939* (Ithaca, NY: Cornell University Press, 1984), 24–25.

17. Görlitz, *The Kaiser and His Court*, 65.

18. Robert B. Asprey, *The German High Command at War: Hindenburg and Ludendorff Conduct World War I* (New York: William Morrow and Co., 1991), 143.

19. Nostitz von Hindenburg, *Hindenburg at Home*, 7, 23.

20. Asprey, *German High Command*, 168.

21. An amusing and telling depiction of "Hindenburgitis, or the Prussian House Beautiful" from *Punch* included Hindenburg planters, lamps, portraits, busts, pillows, and tablecloths. Even the lady of the house is shown wearing a sneering Hindenburg brooch! *Mr. Punch's History of the Great War* (London, Cassell, 1919), 119; reproduced in George L. Mosse, *Fallen Soldiers: Reshaping the Memory of the World Wars* (Oxford: Oxford University Press, 1990), 9.

22. Quoted in Hugo von Freytag-Loringhoven, *The Power of Personality in War* (Harrisburg, PA: The Military Service Publishing Co., 1911, 1955), 38.

23. Actually, the French had pulled forces back from the border, making it clear (especially to Britain) that Germany had first violated Belgian territory.

24. Albert J. Beveridge, *What Is Back of the War* (Indianapolis: The Bobbs-Merrill Co., 1915), 71–78.

25. Görlitz, *The Kaiser and His Court*, 101.

26. Asprey, *German High Command*, 203.

27. Ludwig, *Hindenburg*, 125.

28. At Verdun in 843 A.D. Charlemagne's sons split his empire. During the French Revolution a French commander at Verdun committed suicide in 1792 rather than surrender. In 1870 Verdun was the last border fortress to surrender in the Franco-Prussian War.

29. Quoted in Asprey, *German High Command*, 229.

30. Görlitz, *The Kaiser and His Court*, 188.

31. Charles de Gaulle, *The Enemy's House Divided*, trans. Robert Eden (Chapel Hill: University of North Carolina Press, [1924], 2002), 82.

32. Hew Strachan, "Germany in the First World War: The Problem of Strategy," *German History* 12 (1994): 237–49:240.

*Chapter 3: Supreme Command, 1916–1917*

1. Marion Dönhoff, *Before the Storm: Memories of My Youth in Old Prussia* (New York: Alfred A. Knopf, 1990), 10.

2. Philipp Witkop, ed., *German Students' War Letters* (London: Methuen, 1929; Philadelphia: Pine Street Books, 2002), 256, 372.

3. Hindenburg, *Out of My Life*, 1:266–67.

4. Ground hay became a substitute for flour; turnips mixed with gelatin, water, and various coloring agents formed an ersatz jam; and various types of glue (!) substituted for blancmange (a sweet jelly normally made from corn flour and milk).

5. "A forcible alteration of food habits goes to the very heart of tradition, expectations, and identity," notes Avner Offer in *The First World War: An Agrarian Interpretation* (Oxford: Clarendon Press, 1989), 39.

6. Memorandum to the Imperial Chancellor, September 13, 1916, No. 34647, signed by Hindenburg. The memorandum concluded by declaring, "The whole German nation must live only in the service of the Fatherland."

7. The code name for the withdrawal was *Alberich*, the malicious dwarf of the *Nibelungen*.

8. Britain muddled through the U-boat crisis and reformed its naval strategy, learning that defensive tactics were often more effective than offensive ones in finding and destroying submarines and that destroyers were better used escorting convoys than screening the Grand Fleet.

9. Arden Bucholz, *Hans Delbrück and the German Military Establishment* (Iowa City: University of Iowa Press, 1985), 118.

10. Perhaps German leaders were truly unable to entertain alternatives, concludes Barbara Tuchman. "Character is fate, as the Greeks believed. Germans were schooled in winning objectives by force, unschooled in adjustment. They could not bring themselves to forgo aggrandizement even at the risk of defeat." See Tuchman, *The March of Folly: From Troy to Vietnam* (London: Cardinal, 1984, 1990), 34.

11. Germany's clever introduction of Vladimir I. Lenin as a poison pill into a prostrated Russia administered the coup de grâce to a provisional government that vainly sought to continue the war. Lenin's promise of "bread, peace, land" proved far more attractive to Russian peasants than calls to continue the fight against a superior German army. After the October Revolution, Russia was forced to sue for peace in a process that revealed the worst excesses of Hindenburg and Ludendorff's megalomania.

12. Hindenburg, *Out of My Life*, 1:13.

13. Barbara W. Tuchman, *The Zimmermann Telegram* (New York: Viking, 1958).

14. See Fritz Fischer, *Germany's Aims in the First World War* (New York: W. W. Norton & Co., 1961, 1967), for the sweeping annexations envisioned by the German Program of November 1916 (313–16) and the Kreuznach War Aims Program of April 23, 1917 (346–51). Germany's war aims, already ambitious in 1914, continued to wax as Russian strength waned.

15. On July 31, 1914, Germany declared a state of siege that placed the entire country (Bavaria excepted) under the authority of regional army commanders. Their decisions overrode those made by civilian authorities.

16. Ludendorff, *Ludendorff's Own Story*, 2:57–60. Hindenburg sought a revival of the patriotic enthusiasm exhibited by soldiers and citizens in 1914, hence his support of the Fatherland Party.

17. Martin Kitchen, *The Silent Dictatorship: The Politics of the German High Command under Hindenburg and Ludendorff, 1916–1918* (New York: Holmes & Meier, 1976), 22, 272, and passim.

18. See Alfred Vagts, *A History of Militarism: Civilian and Military* (New York: Meridian Books, 1937, 1959), 248, 262.

19. Surely one of the most stirring and heartrending legacies of World War I was the march of France's *grandes mutilés* on July 14, 1919. See Alistair Horne, *To Lose a Battle: France 1940* (London: Macmillan Publishers, 1969, 1990), 46–53.

20. On December 22, 1917, the Kaiser visited Crown Prince Rupprecht's army group near Cambrai. Addressing the soldiers, Wilhelm said he brought "greetings from the Field Marshal [Hindenburg]." This role reversal alarmed Rupprecht, who noted that subjects convey the sovereign's greeting, not vice versa. Cited in Alan Palmer, *Victory 1918* (New York: Atlantic Monthly Press, 1998), 168.

21. Quoted in Fischer, *Germany's Aims*, 428. The reference to "Now thank we all our God" (*Nun danket alle Gott*) is to the hymn sung by Frederick the Great's army after its victory at Leuthen in 1757, which secured Silesia.

22. Major Gert von Hindenburg (Hindenburg's nephew), *Hindenburg 1847–1934: Soldier and Statesman* (London: Hutchinson & Co., 1935), 57.

*Chapter 4: Collapse and Catastrophe, 1918*

1. For the infantry side of the new tactics, see Bruce I. Gudmundsson, *Stormtroop Tactics: Innovation in the German Army, 1914–1918* (New York: Praeger, 1989), and Timothy T. Lupfer, *The Dynamics of Doctrine: The Changes in German Tactical Doctrine during the First World War* (Fort Leavenworth, KS: Combat Studies Institute, U.S. Army Command and General Staff College, 1981). The artillery side is covered in David T. Zabecki, *Steel Wind: Colonel Georg Bruchmüller and the Birth of Modern Artillery* (Westport, CT: Praeger, 1994).

2. Dennis E. Showalter, "German Grand Strategy: A Contradiction in Terms?" *Militärgeschichtliche Mitteilungen* 58 (1990): 65–102.

3. Holger H. Herwig, "Tunes of Glory at the Twilight Stage: The Bad Homburg Crown Council and the Evolution of German Statecraft, 1917/18," *German Studies Review* 6 (1983): 53–63.

4. The letter is reproduced in *The Causes of the German Collapse in 1918: Sections of the Officially Authorized Report of the Commission of the German Constituent Assembly and of the German Reichstag, 1919–1928* (Hamden, CT: Archon Books, 1969), 25–28.

5. *The Causes of the German Collapse*, 39.

6. Görlitz, *The Kaiser and His Court*, 398. In 1918 Germany maintained armies of occupation in or sent military expeditions to Rumania, the Baltic states, Finland, Batum and Baku, and Odessa. In Ukraine, German divisions propped up the short-lived reactionary regime of Hetman Skoropadsky.

7. Ludendorff, *Ludendorff's Own Story*, 2:215.

8. German soldiers' belt buckles were engraved with *Gott mit uns* (God is with us). For a comprehensive account of the Ludendorff Offensives, see Martin Kitchen, *The German Offensives of 1918* (London: Tempus Publishing Ltd., 2001).

9. Görlitz, *The Kaiser and His Court*, entry for March 23, 1918. The Iron Cross with Golden Rays was also known as the *Blücherkreuz*.

10. John W. Wheeler-Bennett, *Hindenburg: The Wooden Titan* (London: Macmillan, 1936; New York: St. Martin's Press, 1967), 149. During the war Hindenburg wrote more than 1,500 letters to his wife.

11. General Sir Charles Grant, "Some Notes Made at Marshal Foch's Headquarters, August to November, 1918," Grant Papers 3/2, p. 5, Liddell Hart Centre for Military Archives, King's College, London. Our thanks to Michael S. Neiberg for this reference. Prominent German generals and staff officers also criticized Ludendorff for tactical monomania. See Holger H. Herwig, *The First World War: Germany and Austria-Hungary 1914–1918* (London: Arnold, 1997), 409.

12. Hindenburg, *Out of My Life*, 1:124. It was not for lack of steel or labor, as Germany laid down two battle cruisers in 1917: *Mackensen* and *Graf Spee*.

13. Asprey, *German High Command*, 404–05.

14. Wilhelm Deist, "The Military Collapse of the German Empire: The Reality behind the Stab-in-the-Back Myth," *War in History* 3 (1996): 186–207:202. Deist cites as "in no way excessive" Erich-Otto Volkmann's estimate of 750,000 to 1,000,000 shirkers in the last months of the war.

15. Deist, "Military Collapse," 203.

16. Correlli Barnett, *The Swordbearers: Supreme Command in the First World War* (New York: William Morrow and Co., 1964), 342.

17. Richard Bessel, "The Great War in German Memory: The Soldiers of the First World War, Demobilization, and Weimar Political Culture," *German History* 6 (1988), 20–34.

18. See Whalen, *Bitter Wounds*, 30–31.

19. As Bethmann Hollweg noted in 1916, "You don't know Ludendorff, who is only great at a time of success. If things go badly he loses his nerve." Görlitz, *The Kaiser and His Court*, 406.

20. Ludendorff, *Ludendorff's Own Story*, 2:386.

21. Cited in Joseph Gies, *Crisis 1918* (New York: W. W. Norton, 1974), 260.

22. By early October an army corps with seven divisions in its order of battle was reporting its infantry strength at fewer than 5,000 men—less than 10 percent of authorized tables of organization. One regiment counted only 200 men. Another mustered only 120 men, organized in four companies instead of the regulation twelve.

23. Compare with Michael Geyer, "Insurrectionary Warfare: The German Debate about a *Levée en Masse* in October 1918," *Journal of Modern History* 73 (2001): 459–527, and "People's War: The German Debate about a *Levée en Masse* in October 1918," in *The People in Arms: Military Myth and National Mobilization since the French Revolution*, eds. Daniel Moran and Arthur Waldron (Cambridge: Cambridge University Press, 2003), 124–58.

24. Ludendorff, *Ludendorff's Own Story*, 2:423.

25. Ludendorff fled to Sweden, reputedly donning a false beard and blue spectacles as a disguise!

26. For his pains, Erzberger was murdered in 1921 by the rightist "Organization C."

27. Deist, "Military Collapse," 207. More than 12,000 German Jews died for their country in the war, and 35,000 were decorated for bravery. Despite this distinguished record of sacrifice and service, German Jews were nevertheless singled out after the war for persecution, especially by *völkisch* groups driven by "racial" hatreds.

28. *Der Fahneneid ist jetzt nur eine Idee*, Groener said: "Today our oath is just words." But this confession would have been far more telling if it had come from the Prussian Hindenburg.

29. Leonard V. Smith, "Remobilizing the Citizen-Soldier through the French Army Mutinies of 1917," in *State, Society, and*

*Mobilization in Europe during the First World War*, ed. J. Horne (Cambridge: Cambridge University Press, 1997), 144–159.

30. De Gaulle, *The Enemy's House Divided*, 2:51.

31. Cited in Telford Taylor, *Sword and Swastika: Generals and Nazis in the Third Reich* (New York: Simon and Schuster, 1952), 16.

## Chapter 5: Weimar and Hitler

1. Also dismayed, but for different reasons, was Lloyd George, who predicted, "We shall have to do the whole thing over again [war] in twenty-five years at three times the cost."

2. As the French historian Jacques Benoist-Méchin noted, "If Marshal Hindenburg had come himself to hand his sword over to Marshal Foch . . . no doubt Germany would have understood that she was [militarily] beaten. . . . In agreeing to negotiate with Erzberger, we have accorded the General Staff an unexpected immunity and have obliged the young German Republic to assume for itself all the burden of the defeat." Cited in Vagts, *A History of Militarism*, 280.

3. Hitler's wartime grade is nearly always translated as "corporal" in an American context. In fact a *Gefreiter* in the imperial army was the exact counterpart of a private first class in the U.S. army, an ordinary soldier with a little extra, but nothing particularly special, in the way of skill or competence. The grade of corporal was called *Unteroffizier* and a three-stripe sergeant was a *Sergeant.* The confusion about Hitler's status arose when the *Reichswehr*, in a bit of linguistic cleaning, abolished *Unteroffizier* as a "foreign" designation. Instead, to simplify a complex reworking, *Unteroffizieren* were upgraded to sergeant status and *Gefreiter* became corporals, effectively promoting Hitler after the fact.

4. Telford Taylor, *Sword and Swastika*, 33.

5. It was General Sir Neill Malcolm, the head of the British military mission in Berlin, who reputedly offered—at Ludendorff's prompting—the emotive phrase "stab in the back."

6. "Have we been unworthy of our fathers?" Hindenburg, using the royal "we," asked after the war. See *Out of My Life*, 1:35.

7. Deist, "Military Collapse," 200. Widespread criminal behavior and indiscipline characterized some elements of the imperial army at the beginning of the war as well. See John Horne and

Alan Kramer, *German Atrocities, 1914: A History of Denial* (New Haven: Yale University Press, 2001).

8. On the criminalization of German society, driven by economic exigency and manipulative governmental policies, see Gerald Feldman, "Mobilizing Economies for War," in *The Great War and the Twentieth Century*, eds. Jay Winter et al. (New Haven, CT: Yale University Press, 2000), 166–86, esp. 177.

9. By the summer of 1918, those who benefited from the system, notes Wilhelm Deist, "contrasted with the grey mass of the troops. Bitterness about these conditions had become deeply embedded, and the yearning for peace, for an end to the war, was general and strong, undoubtedly also influenced by the political conflicts at home over war aims and the Prussian franchise." Deist, "Military Collapse," 194.

10. De Gaulle as well as Général Buat (in his *Hindenburg: Librairie Chapelot*, 1921) joined Foch in seeing Hindenburg as a patriot. Hindenburg's gravitas and dignity were especially powerful and persuasive within military settings.

11. Neudeck was also put in Oskar's name to avoid inheritance taxes upon his father's death.

12. Hitler systematically used bribes, stolen estates, and tax-free gifts to silence senior *Wehrmacht* leaders, notes Gerhard L. Weinberg. For details, see Norman J. W. Goda, "Black Marks: Hitler's Bribery of His Senior Officers during World War II," *Journal of Modern History* 72 (2000): 413–52, and Gerd R. Ueberschär and Winfried Vogel, *Dienen und Verdienen: Hitlers Geschenke an seine Eliten* (Frankfurt: Ficher Taschenbuch Verlag, 2000). After Neudeck's expansion, in an apparent quid pro quo, Hindenburg honored Hermann Göring, a mere captain in World War I but a senior Nazi, with the honorary rank of infantry general. Another field marshal of World War I vintage who won an estate from Hitler was August von Mackensen, although Mackensen's dotation was public, not secret. Hitler "won my heart as a statesman, soldier, and man," gushed Mackensen in 1933. See John Lukacs, *The Hitler of History* (New York: Alfred A. Knopf, 1997), 216.

13. "Foreign News. Germany," *Time Magazine* 24 (July 16, 1934): 17.

14. *Berlin in Lights: The Diaries of Count Harry Kessler (1918–1937)*, trans. and ed. Charles Kessler, introduction by Ian Buruma (New York: Grove Press, 1999), 267.

15. He shared this assessment with Churchill. See Winston S. Churchill, *The Gathering Storm*, vol. 1 of *The Second World War* (Boston: Houghton Mifflin Co., 1948), 25.

16. Germany had half a million widows after the war, most of whom did not remarry.

17. See Robert M. Citino, *The Path to Blitzkrieg: Doctrine and Training in the German Army, 1920–1939* (Boulder, CO: Lynne Rienner, 1999), 137–38.

18. Gert von Hindenburg, *Hindenburg*, 244–45.

19. Donald J. Goodspeed, *Ludendorff: Genius of World War I* (Boston: Houghton Mifflin Co., 1966), 306–07.

20. Stresemann shared the Nobel Peace Prize with France's foreign minister, Aristide Briand, in 1926 for creating the "spirit of Locarno," a spirit representing an "almost unprecedented attempt to base politics on the principle of mutual friendship and trust," in the words of Fridtjof Nansen, 1922's peace laureate.

21. Prominent *Reichswehr* leaders supported the Nazis from their early days, providing funds that the Nazis used to buy the *Völkischer Beobachter*, the Nazi party newspaper.

22. Schleicher, like Oskar, was a veteran of the Third Regiment of the Foot Guards.

23. Weterstetten and Watson, *Hindenburg*, 253.

24. The nationalist Stresemann had in 1924 referred to the army as a *Wallenstein soldateska* (a reference to private, mercenary soldiers of the 1620s and 1630s) and also as "a kind of Praetorian guard divorced from and in opposition to the mass of the people." See F. L. Carsten, *Britain and the Weimar Republic: The British Documents* (New York: Schocken Books, 1984), 181–82.

25. Martin Broszat, *Hitler and the Collapse of Weimar Germany* (New York: Berg, 1987), 19–20.

26. Konrad Heiden, *The Führer* (New York: Carroll & Graf Publishers, 1944, 1999), 336. The joke was also a euphemism: Hitler could lick Hindenburg's backside—"kiss his ass" in colloquial English.

27. Heiden, *The Führer*, 344.

28. Carsten, *Britain and the Weimar Republic*, 253.

29. *Ich hatt' einen Kameraden* was a reference to a popular soldiers' song.

30. To those who expressed concern about Hitler's tractability, Papen replied, "What are you worried about? I have Hindenburg's confidence. In two months we shall have Hitler squeezed into a corner so that he squeaks." See Joachim C. Fest, *The Face of the Third Reich: Portraits of the Nazi Leadership* (New York: Pantheon Books, 1970), 157.

31. Even the savvy Lloyd George, after visiting with Hitler, wrote that he was a "born leader" who wanted only to defend Germany. "The establishment of a German hegemony in Europe," Lloyd George concluded in 1936, "is not even on the horizon of Nazism." See Frank Owen, *Tempestuous Journey: Lloyd George His Life and Times* (New York: McGraw-Hill, 1955), 736.

32. Quoted in Ian Kershaw, *Hitler 1889–1936: Hubris* (New York: W. W. Norton, 1998), 377. Hugenberg, the nationalist leader, also had second thoughts, saying on January 31, "Yesterday I committed the worst folly of my life: I became the ally of the greatest demagogue in world history." Quoted in Andreas Dorpalen, *Hindenburg and the Weimar Republic* (Princeton, NJ: Princeton University Press, 1964), 445.

33. Wheeler-Bennett, *Hindenburg*, 308.

34. Wheeler-Bennett, *Hindenburg*, 442. Jokes of this sort, if overheard by the wrong person, could end with the teller doing hard labor in the new Nazi concentration camps.

35. George Clare, *Last Waltz in Vienna: The Rise and Destruction of a Family, 1842–1942* (New York: Owl Books, 1981, 1989), 121. Clare later served in the British army during World War II and in Berlin after the war, an experience he recounts in *Before the Wall: Berlin Days 1946–1948* (New York: Penguin, 1989).

36. Victor Klemperer, *I Will Bear Witness: A Diary of the Nazi Years, 1933–1941* (New York: Random House, 1998), 8, 11.

37. Klemperer, *I Will Bear Witness*, 22. The reference came on June 29, 1933.

38. Walther Hubatsch, *Hindenburg und der Staat: Aus den Papieren des Generalfeldmarschalls und Reichspräsidenten von 1878 bis 1934* (Göttingen: Musterschmidt-Verlag, 1966), 376–77.

39. Henry Friedlander, *The Origins of Nazi Genocide: From Euthanasia to the Final Solution* (Chapel Hill: University of North Carolina Press, 1995).

40. It is not known who wrote and approved this telegram. It had an impact, noted Albert Speer, who wrote, "That Hitler's action was approved by this supreme judge [Hindenburg] was highly reassuring." Like many Germans of his class, Speer saw Hindenburg as "the symbol of authority," a "strong, steadfast hero" who "seemed to belong to a somewhat legendary realm." See Speer, *Inside the Third Reich*, 52.

41. Steven Aschheim, *The Nietzsche Legacy in Germany: 1890–1990* (Berkeley: University of California Press, 1993), 234. Our thanks to Robert C. Pirro for this reference.

42. "I swear before God this sacred oath: I will render unconditional obedience to Adolf Hitler, the Führer of the German nation and people, Supreme Commander of the Armed Forces, and will be ready as a brave soldier to risk my life at any time for this oath."

*Epilogue*

1. As Holger Herwig provocatively asked, "Is it too far off the mark to suggest that the 'twisted road to Auschwitz' began with the *Dolchstoßlegende*?" Herwig, "Of Men and Myths: The Use and Abuse of History and the Great War," in *The Great War and the Twentieth Century*, eds. Jay Winter et al. (New Haven, CT: Yale University Press, 2000), 299–330: on 323.

2. "As soon as I am recognized on the street, the traffic is held up," Hindenburg complained after the war. Even a stroll with his wife ended with him "being held up by crowds of warm-hearted Hanoverians." See Gert von Hindenburg, *Hindenburg*, 196.

3. Churchill, *The Gathering Storm*, 52.

# Bibliographic Note

T HIS NOTE focuses on sources available in English and those most readily accessible to readers with access to a college or large public library. It is not exhaustive; nor does it include all sources cited in the notes.

An understanding of Hindenburg begins with his own apologia: Paul von Hindenburg, *Aus meinem Leben*, translated as *Out of My Life*, 2 vols. (New York: Harper & Bros., 1921). Hindenburg's published memoirs for 1911 to 1934 provide limited insight into the man himself as they were written by Colonel Hermann Mertz von Quirnheim of the Potsdam Reichsarchiv. Walther Hubatsch cleansed Hindenburg's private papers in the 1960s. On these points see Holger H. Herwig, "Of Men and Myths: The Use and Abuse of History and the Great War," in *The Great War and the Twentieth Century*, eds. Jay Winter et al. (New Haven, CT: Yale University Press, 2000), 299–330, 305. Nevertheless, the Hubatsch collection remains useful: Walther Hubatsch, *Hindenburg und der Staat: Aus den Papieren des Generalfeldmarschalls und Reichspräsidenten von 1878 bis 1934* (Berlin: Musterschmidt, 1966).

Useful too are the highly selective accounts of Erich Ludendorff, who believed himself betrayed by Hindenburg in the closing stages of the war. See *Ludendorff's Own Story, August 1914– November 1918: The Great War from the Siege of Liège to the Signing of the Armistice as Viewed from the Grand Headquarters of the German Army*, 2 vols. (New York: Harper and Brothers, 1919), and *The General Staff and Its Problems: The History of the Relations between the High Command and the German Imperial*

*Government as Revealed by Official Documents,* 2 vols. (New York: E. P. Dutton and Co., 1920). For rival perspectives, see Erich von Falkenhayn, *General Headquarters, 1914–1916, and Its Critical Decisions* (London: Hutchinson, 1919), and Max Hoffmann, *The War of Lost Opportunities* (London: Battery Press, Imperial War Museum, 1999).

The most engaging and critical biography of Hindenburg is by John W. Wheeler-Bennett, *Hindenburg: The Wooden Titan* (London: Macmillan, 1936; New York: St. Martin's Press, 1967). Based on considerable firsthand knowledge of political intrigue in Weimar, Wheeler-Bennett's account gained the distinction of being banned in Nazi Germany. Also important are Andreas Dorpalen, *Hindenburg and the Weimar Republic* (Princeton, NJ: Princeton University Press, 1964), and Rudolf Olden, *Hindenburg: Oder der Geist der preussischen Armee* (Nurnberg: Nest-Verlag, 1948; Hildesheim, 1982). Walter Görlitz, *Hindenburg: Ein Lebensbild* (Bonn, Athenäum, 1953), interprets Hindenburg as an embodiment of Prussian tradition; Emil Ludwig, *Hindenburg* (Chicago: The John C. Winston Co., 1935) is an exercise in Marxist-Freudian debunking.

The rise to power of national socialism generated a spate of popular works focused on Hindenburg. Gerhard Schultze-Pfaelzer, *Hindenburg: Peace, War, Aftermath* (London: P. Allan, 1931); Rudolph Weterstetten and A. M. K. Watson, *The Biography of President von Hindenburg* (New York: The Macmillan Co., 1930); Margaret Goldsmith and Frederick Voigt, *Hindenburg: The Man and the Legend* (New York: William Morrow & Co., 1930); Helene Nostitz von Hindenburg (Hindenburg's niece), *Hindenburg at Home: An Intimate Biography* (New York: Duffield & Green, 1931); Thomas Russell Ybarra, *Hindenburg: The Man with Three Lives* (New York: Duffield & Green, 1932); and Major Gert von Hindenburg (Hindenburg's nephew), *Hindenburg 1847–1934: Soldier and Statesman* (London: Hutchinson & Co., 1935), offer unfamiliar details, but are otherwise unremarkable.

Hindenburg is usually reduced to a cipher in various biographies of Ludendorff, yet they remain essential reading. See Donald J. Goodspeed, *Ludendorff: Genius of World War I* (Boston: Houghton Mifflin Co., 1966); Roger Parkinson, *Tormented Warrior: Ludendorff and the Supreme Command* (New York: Stein and Day, 1978); and Karl Tschuppik, *Ludendorff: The Tragedy of a Specialist* (Westport, CT: Greenwood Press, 1932, 1975). Broader studies of the German general staff are provided by Gordon Craig, *The Politics of the Prussian Army, 1640–1945* (Oxford: Clarendon Press, 1955); Walter Görlitz, *History of the German General Staff, 1657–1945* (New York: Praeger, 1953); and John W. Wheeler-Bennett, *The Nemesis of Power: The German Army in Politics, 1918–1945* (New York: Viking Press, 1967).

For the defining event that generated the Hindenburg legend, see Dennis E. Showalter, *Tannenberg: Clash of Empires* (Hamden, CT: Archon Books, 1991; Dulles, VA: Brassey's, 2004). A counterpoint is provided by Theo Schwarzmüller, *Zwischen Kaiser und "Führer": Generalfeldmarschall August von Mackensen: Eine politische Biographie* (Paderborn: Schèoningh, 1995). Useful for its clear maps and concise campaign summary is John Sweetman, *Tannenberg 1914* (London: Cassell and Co., 2002).

The Eastern and Balkan fronts in World War I remain understudied, in part because neither the Austro-Hungarian successor states nor Bolshevik Russia saw a need to publicize heroics on these fronts. The best account in English remains Norman Stone's *The Eastern Front, 1914–1917* (New York: Scribner, 1975). An essential study that stresses Germany's inability to forge an effective coalition with Austria-Hungary, leading eventually to a heavy-handed German takeover, is Holger H. Herwig, *The First World War: Germany and Austria-Hungary, 1914–1918* (New York: St. Martin's Press, 1997).

On the fatal partnership between Hindenburg and Ludendorff from 1916 to 1918, see Martin Kitchen, *The Silent Dictatorship: The Politics of the German High Command under Hindenburg and Ludendorff, 1916–1918* (New York: Holmes & Meier, 1976); Robert B. Asprey, *The German High Command at*

*War: Hindenburg and Ludendorff Conduct World War I* (New York: William Morrow and Co., 1991); and Trevor N. Dupuy, *The Military Lives of Hindenburg and Ludendorff of Imperial Germany* (New York: Franklin Watts, Inc., 1970). Charles de Gaulle's perceptive account of Germany's military defeat, which blamed Hindenburg and especially Ludendorff for Germany's stunning moral collapse in 1918, is now available in English: *The Enemy's House Divided*, translated by Robert Eden (Chapel Hill: University of North Carolina Press, 1924, 2002).

Holger Afflerbach's *Falkenhayn: Politisches Denken und Handeln im Kaiserreich* (Munich: Oldenbourg, 1994) is excellent from the perspective of Hindenburg and Ludendorff's principal military rival. On Falkenhayn's predecessor, see Annika Mombauer, *Helmuth von Moltke and the Origins of the First World War* (Cambridge: Cambridge University Press, 2001). On the kaiser himself, see Lamar Cecil, *Wilhelm II*, 2 vols. (Chapel Hill: University of North Carolina Press, 1989–1996), and Thomas Kohut, *Wilhelm II and the Germans* (Oxford: Oxford University Press, 1991). On Bethmann Hollweg, see Konrad Jarausch, *The Enigmatic Chancellor: Bethmann Hollweg and the Hubris of Imperial Germany* (New Haven, CT: Yale University Press, 1973). Addressing imperial Germany's military demise is Rod Paschall, *The Defeat of Imperial Germany, 1917–1918* (Chapel Hill, NC: Algonquin Books, 1989).

Roger Chickering's *Imperial Germany and the Great War, 1914–1918* (New York: Cambridge University Press, 1998) is a model of conciseness and insight. On German militarism, see the classic account of Gerhard Ritter, *The Sword and the Scepter: The Problem of Militarism in Germany*, 4 vols. (Coral Gables, FL: University of Miami Press, 1969–1973). On the Hindenburg Program, see Gerald D. Feldman, *Army, Industry and Labor in Germany, 1914–1918* (Princeton, NJ: Princeton University Press, 1966), and Robert B. Armeson, *Total Warfare and Compulsory Labor: A Study of the Military-Industrial Complex in Germany during World War I* (The Hague: M. Nijhoff, 1964).

General accounts of World War I are legion. Sir Michael

Howard provides an incisive overview in *The First World War* (Oxford: Oxford University Press, 2002). Already indispensable is the first volume of Hew Strachan's projected three-volume history of the war: *To Arms,* vol. 1 of *The First World War* (Oxford: Oxford University Press, 2001). Two authors who have generated controversy by attacking French and British operations and tactics on the western front while praising German military performance are Niall Ferguson, *The Pity of War: Explaining World War I* (New York: Basic Books, 1999), and John Mosier, *The Myth of the Great War: How the Germans Won the Battles and How the Americans Saved the Allies* (New York: HarperCollins, 2001). An older, but still useful, summary of high command in the war that includes a study of Ludendorff is Correlli Barnett, *The Swordbearers: Supreme Command in the First World War* (New York: William Morrow and Co., 1964).

On the mendacious and cynical *Dolchstoßlegende* (stab-in-the-back myth) embraced and advanced by Hindenburg, see Wilhelm Deist, "The Military Collapse of the German Empire: The Reality behind the Stab-in-the-Back Myth," *War in History*, 3 (1996): 186–207, and Joachim Petzold, *Die Dolchstoßlegende: Eine Geschichtsfälschung im Dienst des deutschen Imperialismus und Militarismus* (Berlin: Akademie-Verlag, 1963). German self-deception predates the 1918 collapse, as demonstrated by Holger H. Herwig, "Clio Deceived: Patriotic Self-Censorship in Germany in the Great War," *International Security*, 12 (Fall 1987): 5–44. On the OHL's use of propaganda, see David Welch, *Germany, Propaganda and Total War, 1914–1918* (Newark, NJ: Rutgers University Press, 2000).

The Weimar Republic has drawn historians as a flame draws moths. An evenhanded account is Richard Bessel, *Germany after the First World War* (Oxford: Clarendon Press, 1993). Older but still worth consulting is Arthur Rosenberg, *The Birth of the German Republic, 1871–1918* (Oxford: Oxford University Press, 1931; New York: Russell & Russell, 1962). Francis L. Carsten considers the German army's intimate involvement in Weimar in *The Reichswehr and Politics: 1918–1933* (Oxford: Clarendon

Press, 1966). On the events leading up to Hindenburg's tragic embrace of Hitler, see Henry Ashby Turner, Jr., *Hitler's Thirty Days to Power: January 1933* (London: Addison-Wesley, 1996); Theodor Eschenburg, "The Role of the Personality in the Crisis of the Weimar Republic: Hindenburg, Brüning, Groener, Schleicher," in *Republic to Reich: The Making of the Nazi Revolution,* ed. Hajo Holborn (New York: Pantheon Books, 1972), 3–50; Ian Kershaw, *Hitler, 1889–1936: Hubris* (New York: W. W. Norton & Co., 1999); and Richard J. Evans, *The Coming of the Third Reich* (New York: Penguin Press, 2004).

# Index

Aisne offensive. *See* Ludendorff Offensives

American Expeditionary Forces (AEF), x, 62, 66

Amiens (August 1918), 67

Article 231. *See* Versailles, Treaty of

Austria, 6–7, 9, 13, 25, 30, 32, 35–37, 46, 55–57, 65, 74, 101

Austro-Prussian War, 6

Bad Homburg, 54

Barnett, Correlli, 66

Bauer, Max, 41, 49

Belgium, 16, 24, 31, 53, 77, 109

Belleau Wood, 62

Bernhardi, Friedrich von, 15

Beseler, Hans von, 32

Bethmann Hollweg, Theobald von, x, 16, 37, 47–49, 123

Beveridge, Albert J., 30–31

Bismarck, Otto von, 4, 7, 9–10, 47, 56

Blackshirts (SS), 92

Blomberg, Werner von, 99

Blücher, Gebhard Leberecht von, 5, 58

Bohemian Corporal. *See* Hitler, Adolf

Bolshevism, xi, 56, 73, 77–78, 81

Bonaparte, Napoleon, 3–5, 8, 18, 23, 30, 58

Brest-Litovsk, Treaty of, x, 55

British Expeditionary Force (BEF), 45, 53, 58–59, 66

British Fifth Army, 58

British Fourth Army, 69

British Third Army, 69

Brownshirts (SA), 90–91, 93, 98

Brüning, Heinrich, 89, 91–93

Brusilov, Alexei, 36–37

Bucharest, Treaty of, 55

*Burgfrieden,* 48

Cannae, Battle of, 20, 32, 46

Caporetto, Battle of, 45, 53

Central Powers, 32–33, 35, 43, 55, 75

Champagne/Marne offensive. *See* Ludendorff Offensives

Château-Thierry, 62

Churchill, Winston, 36, 104

Clare, George, 97

Clausewitz, Carl von, 13, 47, 56, 74

Clemenceau, Georges, 56, 74

concentration camps, 96, 98–99

Cooper, James Fenimore, 5
Cossacks, 16

Dawes Plan, 83
De Gaulle, Charles, 38, 74, 116,
    123
Delbrück, Hans, ix
*Diktat. See* Versailles, Treaty of
*Dolchstoßlegende*, x, 58, 72, 80–81,
    103, 105, 115, 119, 124
Dönhoff, Marion, 39
Doullens conference, 59

East Prussia, x, 10, 16, 18–19, 23,
    25, 28, 32
Eastern Front, 14–15, 17, 26, 37,
    87, 101
Ebert, Friedrich, 73, 78, 83
Einem, Karl von, 81
*Einkreisung*, 12
Elizabeth, Queen of Prussia, 6
Enabling Act, 97
*Endkampf*, 70
Entente, x, 23, 36–37, 40, 43–46,
    54, 56–57, 59–61, 63, 65,
    67–70, 74–75, 77, 79, 82,
    102
epidemics, 33, 63
Erzberger, Matthias, 72

Falkenhayn, Erich von, x, 23–24,
    26–28, 32–38, 43, 123
Fatherland Party, 47–48, 108, 111
First Ypres, Battle of, 24, 27
Foch, Ferdinand, 46, 56, 59–61,
    65–67, 77, 79, 81, 107, 116
food, shortage of, 41–42, 50, 110
Fourteen Points. *See* Wilson,
    Woodrow
France, 7–9, 13, 16, 20, 23, 30–31,
    33, 35, 45, 52, 56–57, 61, 69,
    74, 77, 87
Franco-Prussian War, 13, 24, 101
Franz Josef, Emperor, 30
Frederick II, 3, 5, 33, 96
*Freikorps*, 78, 89
French army, mutiny of (1917),
    45, 53, 74
French First Army, 69
French Fourth Army, 63
French Sixth Army, 62
Frick, Wilhelm, 94

Galicia, 25, 32–33, 36
German army, morale of, 36–37,
    39–40, 50–51, 58, 62–63,
    66–68, 71, 73–75, 81, 113,
    116
German General Staff, x, 4, 9, 11,
    16–18, 23–24, 27, 32, 37, 39,
    48, 66, 79, 101, 122
German Eighth Army, 11, 17–19,
    23
German Ninth Army, 23, 25
German Third Army, 81
Gneisenau, August von, 5
Goebbels, Joseph, 91, 95, 98
Göring, Hermann, 94, 116
Gorlice-Tarnów offensive, 32
Gough, Hubert, 58
Great Britain, 9, 16, 23, 30–31, 33,
    44–47, 53, 56, 61, 73–74, 87,
    110
Great Depression, 88–89
Groener, Wilhelm, 41, 54, 72–73,
    78, 114
Gumbinnen, Battle of, 17, 20

Haig, Douglas, 56, 59, 61
Hart, Basil Liddell, 18

Heiden, Konrad, 92
Hertling, Georg von, 55, 68, 70
*Hilfsdienstgesetz*, 42
Himmler, Heinrich, 92
Hindenburg Line, 43–45, 63, 68–69
Hindenburg, Oskar von, 9–10, 12, 86, 88–89, 94
Hindenburg, Otto Frederick von, 3
Hindenburg, Paul von, and Austro-Prussian War, 6–7; and Bethmann Hollweg, x, 48–50; character of, ix, 4–5, 10, 18, 26, 29–31, 34–35, 56, 65, 94, 101–105, 109; made Chief of the General Staff, 37–38; childhood of, 3–6; criticism of Austria-Hungary, 25; death of, 99–100; death of wife, 82; and *Dolchstoßlegende*, x–xi, 58, 69, 80–81, 103; election of 1925, x, 83–86; election of 1932, 91–92, 104; and Falkenhayn, 23, 26–28, 33–34, 37–38; and Franco-Prussian War, 7–8; 13, 101; and Hitler, ix, 82, 92–99, 104–105, 117, 125; as icon of militarism, xi, 38, 75, 105; image of, x, 8, 22–23, 28–30, 37, 39–40, 75, 86, 88, 97, 109, 119; and Ludendorff, x, 5, 18–19, 26, 47–48, 51–52, 54–57, 60, 63–72, 95, 102, 109; marriage, 9; military decorations of, 7, 22, 32, 58, 113; Nazi criticism of, 91; and Neudeck, 82; and Oskar, 9, 12, 86, 88, 94; and Papen, 92, 94; pasttimes of, 12, 34, 82, 104; 107; promotion to field marshal, 26; and religion, 4, 29; as substitute kaiser, ix, 49, 86; and Tannenberg, ix–x, 19–22; and Tannenberg Memorial, 83, 87; and Treaty of Versailles, 78–80; views on war, 12–15, 31, 46, 61; and Wilhelm I, 10, 86; and Wilhelm II, x, 11, 28–29, 47–51, 55, 71–73, 101, 112; wooden statues of, 23, 30, 101, 104, 108
Hindenburg Program, x, 40–42, 116, 123
Hintze, Paul von, 63
Hitler, Adolf, ix–xi, 23, 65, 75, 77, 82–83, 87, 89–99, 103–104, 106, 115, 125
Hitler, Alois, 92
Hoffmann, Max, 19, 33–34, 83
Holtzendorff, Henning von, 44
Horthy, Miklós, 78
Hötzendorf, Franz Conrad von, 25, 32, 35–37
Hugenberg, Alfred, 88

Italy, 6, 13, 32, 35, 37, 45, 63, 77, 93

Jewish war record, 67, 81, 98, 114
Joffre, Joseph, 30
*Junkers*, 3–4, 6, 24, 101
Jutland, Battle of, 44

Kahr, Gustav von, 99
Kapp, Wolfgang, 47, 87
Karl, Emperor, 65

Kessler, Harry, 84
Kipling, Rudyard, 16
Kitchener, Earl, 30
Klemperer, Victor, 97–98
*Kohlrübenwinter*, 42
Königgrätz, Battle of, 6, 7, 13
*Konzentrationslager. See* concentration camps
*Kriegsakademie*, 9
Kühlmann, Richard von, 63
*Kulturkampf*, 9

League of Nations, 87
Lenin, Vladimir, 111
Lessing, Theodor, 84
Liebknecht, Karl, 73, 78
Lloyd George, David, 56, 74, 79, 86, 115, 118
Locarno, Treaty of, 87
Lódz, 26
Lubbe, Marinus van der, 96
Ludendorff, Erich, books on, 120–124; character of, 13, 18, 113–114; early career of, 17–18; and Hindenburg, x, 5, 17–19, 22–27, 32–35, 38, 49–57, 60–72, 74–75, 80–81, 83–84, 87, 101–102; and Hindenburg Line, 43–44; Hindenburg Program, 40–43; and Hitler, 83, 95
Ludendorff Offensives, x, 57–65
*Lusitania*, 44
Luxembourg, 16, 77
Luxemburg, Rosa, 78
Lyncker, Moritz von, 37
Lys offensive. *See* Ludendorff Offensives

Mackensen, August von, 32–33, 43, 116

Mann, Thomas, 54
Marne, Second Battle of, 63
Marx, Wilhelm, 83
masculinity, 13, 29
Masurian Lakes, First Battle of, x, 20, 23, 27, 101
Masurian Lakes, Second Battle of, 28
*Materialschlacht*, 40, 45
Meissner, Otto, 88–89, 94, 96
Mexico, 47
Michaelis, Georg, 49, 55
militarism, ix, xi, 15–16, 28, 31, 55, 74–76, 81, 90, 99, 105, 123
Moltke, Helmuth von (the elder), 4, 6–8, 80
Moltke, Helmuth von (the younger), 17, 23
Müller, Georg Alexander von, 56
Müller, Hermann, 89

Napoleon III, 7–8
Nazi. *See* NSDAP
Nernst, Walter, 45
Neudeck, 3, 82, 97, 99, 116
Nietzsche, Friedrich, 99
Nivelle, Robert, 45
Noyon/Montdidier offensive. *See* Ludendorff Offensives
NSDAP (Nazi), ix, xi, 72, 75, 81, 83–84, 88–99, 104

*Oberste Heeresleitung*, 17, 23–24, 28, 32, 49, 50, 61–62, 65, 67, 69, 72, 74
Operation Michael. *See* Ludendorff Offensives
*Osthilfe*, 88, 93

Papen, Franz von, 89, 92–94, 118

Paris Commune, 8
Passchendaele. *See* Third Ypres, Battle of
Pershing, John, 62, 79
Pétain, Henri-Philippe, 36, 59
Pitsudski, Józef, 78
Pius IX, 9
Poland, 23, 26, 32–33, 44, 52, 78
Potsdam, Day of (1933), 96
*Pour le Mérite*, 17, 22, 32
Prince Max of Baden, 70–73
Prusso-Danish War, 6

*Realpolitik*, 4
Reichstag, 23, 42, 47, 49, 50, 52, 65, 69, 70, 73, 89, 92–93, 96–97, 99
Reichstag fire, 96
*Reichswehr*, 87, 90–92, 94, 97–98
Richthofen, Manfred von, 86
Röhm, Ernst, 99
Rommel, Erwin, 90
Roosevelt, Theodore, 12
Rosenberg, Alfred, 99
Rumania, 37, 43, 55–56, 69, 77
Rundstedt, Gerd von, 92
Russia, x, 9, 13, 16, 20, 23–26, 28, 32–33, 35, 37, 44–45, 51–56, 69, 74, 77, 111
Russian First Army, 17, 20, 23
Russian Second Army, 20
Russian Tenth Army, 28
Russian troops, behavior of, 33–34

Scheffer-Boyadel, Reinhard von, 26
Schleicher, Kurt von, 88–89, 91–93, 99
Schlieffen, Alfred von, 9–11, 20, 23
Schlieffen Plan, 16, 23, 54
Schoenaich, Freiherr von, 76
Scipio Africanus, 107
Second Reich, ix, xi, 8, 11, 13, 38, 47, 101–103
Seeckt, Hans von, 87
Serbia, 25
Siegfried Line. *See* Hindenburg Line
Socialism, in Germany, 48–49, 67, 69, 73, 81, 89, 92, 97, 104
Somme, Battle of, 36–37, 39–40
Spartacists, 73, 78
Speer, Albert, 23, 108, 119
Sperling, Gertrud Wilhelmine von (Hindenburg's wife), 9, 18, 28, 58, 82, 99
St. Privat, 7
*Stahlhelm*, 95
Strachan, Hew, 38
Stresemann, Gustav, 83, 87–88, 117
submarine wafare, x, 45, 53, 59, 62, 80, 102, 110
*Sussex*, 44

tanks, 61, 67
Tannenberg, Battle of, ix–x, 10, 20, 22–23, 27, 36, 38, 68, 71–72, 80, 83, 99, 101, 108
Tannenberg Memorial, 87, 99
Teutonic knights, 3, 22
Thaer, Albrecht von, 61–62
Third Foot Guards, 6, 8, 96
Third Ypres (Passchendaele), Battle of, 45, 54
Tirpitz, Alfred von, 44, 47, 83
Torgau, Battle of, 3

Treitschke, Heinrich von, 15
Trotsky, Leon, 55

U-boats. *See* submarine warfare
United States, x, 41, 44–46, 54,
    57, 73, 75, 83, 89, 102

*Vaterländischer Unterricht*, 50
Verdun, x, 35–37, 39–40, 43, 60,
    110
Versailles, x, 8
Versailles, Treaty of, 76–80, 87,
    90, 102
Vogel, Hugo, 30, 34

war enthusiasm, myth of (1914),
    15–16, 107–108
*Wehrmacht*, 87, 99, 116
Weimar Republic, ix, xi, 9,
    77–79, 82, 88–89, 93,
    103–104, 124–125
*Weltpolitik*, 10, 52
Western Front, x, 23–24, 26, 31,
    39–40, 43, 53–54, 65, 69, 102
Wilhelm I, 8, 10, 86
Wilhelm II, ix–x, 3, 7–12, 16–18,
    22–24, 26, 28–29, 31–33,
    37–38, 43, 45, 47–49, 51–56,
    58, 70–73, 75, 82, 84, 87, 97,
    101–102, 104, 112, 123
Wilhelm, Crown Prince, 35, 73
Wilson, Woodrow, 45, 55, 70–71,
    79, 86

Young Plan, 91

Zimmermann Telegram, 46, 75

# About the Authors

William J. Astore, lieutenant colonel, United States Air Force (USAF) is associate provost and dean of students at the Defense Language Institute Foreign Language Center, Presidio of Monterey, California. He earned his doctorate in modern history from the University of Oxford in 1996. He has taught military history at the Naval Postgraduate School and at the USAF Academy, where he was an associate professor. This is his second book. He lives in Pebble Beach, California.

Dennis E. Showalter is professor of history at Colorado College in Colorado Springs, Colorado. He earned his doctorate in history from the University of Minnesota in 1969. His numerous books include *The Wars of Frederick the Great* (1996), *Tannenberg: Clash of Empires* (1991, 2004), and *Railroads and Rifles: Soldiers, Technology and the Unification of Germany* (1975). His most recent book is *The Wars of German Unification* (2004). A former president of the Society for Military History, he has also taught at both the United States Military Academy and the USAF Academy. He lives in Colorado Springs, Colorado.

MILITARY PROFILES
AVAILABLE

*Farragut: America's First Admiral*
 Robert J. Schneller, Jr.
*Drake: For God, Queen, and Plunder*
 Wade G. Dudley
*Santa Anna: A Curse upon Mexico*
 Robert L. Scheina
*Eisenhower: Soldier-Statesman of the American Century*
 Douglas Kinnard
*Semmes: Rebel Raider*
 John M. Taylor
*Doolittle: Aerospace Visionary*
 Dik Alan Daso
*Foch: Supreme Allied Commander in the Great War*
 Michael S. Neiberg
*Villa: Soldier of the Mexican Revolution*
 Robert L. Scheina
*Cushing: Civil War SEAL*
 Robert J. Schneller, Jr.
*Alexander: Invincible King of Macedonia*
 Peter G. Tsouras
*Franco: Soldier, Commander, Dictator*
 Geoffrey Jensen
*Forrest: The Confederacy's Relentless Warrior*
 Robert M. Browning, Jr.
*Meade: Victor of Gettysburg*
 Richard A. Sauers

## MILITARY PROFILES
## FORTHCOMING

*Halsey*
  Robert J. Cressman
*Tirpitz*
  Michael Epkenhans
*Petain*
  Robert B. Bruce
*Winfield Scott*
  Samuel Watson
*Benedict Arnold*
  Mark Hayes

11/06